VEG BOX

VEG BOX (CONTINUED)

Asparagus
166, 184

Aubergines
72, 83, 146

Avocados
184

Beetroot
106

Brussels sprouts
99

Butternut squash
91, 163

Cabbage
92, 158

Carrots
64, 68, 92, 117, 143, 212

Cauliflower
179

Celeriac
106

Celery
143

Courgettes
75, 81, 95, 154

Cucumber
76

Fennel bulbs
95

Ginger
36, 42, 44, 59, 67, 72, 105, 110, 125, 154, 163, 212

Jalapeños
128, 199

Kale
99, 136

Lettuce
166, 184, 195

Mushrooms
106, 127

Onions
16, 24, 32, 34, 38, 42, 52, 56, 64, 67, 68, 71, 72, 76, 83, 84, 92, 99, 106, 110, 114, 117, 122, 125, 127, 128, 131, 141, 143, 144, 146, 149, 157, 163, 166, 169, 170, 184, 188, 199, 200

Oyster mushrooms
127

Parsnips
96

Peppers
48, 76, 128, 153, 166, 199

Porcini mushrooms
106, 127

Potatoes
78, 131, 158, 165, 166, 170, 196, 200

Radishes
64, 182

Shallots
44, 95, 136, 141, 158

Spinach
48, 56, 119, 120, 125

Spring onions
36, 45, 48, 64, 68, 71, 72, 127, 149, 153, 158, 182

Sugar snap peas
64

Swede
106

Sweet potatoes
84

Sweetcorn
59, 184, 199

Swiss chard
38

Tomatoes
15, 24, 28, 48, 56, 67, 72, 76, 81, 86, 88, 105, 106, 114, 125, 128, 143, 146, 149, 154, 157, 163, 169, 184, 188

SPICES

Allspice
56, 96, 125, 144

Asafoetida
59

Berbere spice
117

Black mustard seeds
42, 59, 72, 110, 163

Caraway seeds
149

Cardamom pods
16, 71, 110, 125, 157, 188, 217

Chaat masala
32

Chilli flakes
27, 36, 38, 44, 52, 68, 76, 83, 86, 105, 114, 145, 150, 157, 165, 188, 236

Chilli powder
105

Chillies
15, 32, 38, 42, 44, 52, 56, 59, 72, 76, 92, 96, 105, 110, 120, 125, 127, 136, 143, 145, 146, 149, 153, 154, 163, 165, 169, 184, 193, 200, 236

Cinnamon
41, 56, 59, 110, 127, 144, 157, 212, 224

Cloves
16, 59, 110, 212

Coriander seeds
15, 16, 48, 68, 75, 83, 105, 128, 165

Cumin
16, 27, 38, 52, 59, 64, 68, 71, 72, 83, 84, 92, 105, 110, 125, 141, 144, 149, 153, 157, 163, 188, 196, 200

Curry leaves
42, 92, 163

Curry powder
38, 179

Fennel seeds
95, 166

SPICES (CONTINUED)

Fenugreek seeds
16

Garam masala
42, 72, 154, 163

Nigella seeds
165

Nutmeg
91, 224

Paprika
27, 78, 146, 150, 158, 200

Peppercorns
95, 110

Saffron
71, 75

Star anise
41, 44, 125, 127, 204, 240

Sumac
52, 119, 131, 170

Szechuan peppercorns
44

Turmeric
16, 32, 34, 38, 42, 59, 64, 68, 71, 72, 92, 105, 141, 154, 157, 163, 196

Za'atar
27, 28, 119, 141, 182

MEAT, SEAFOOD & DAIRY

Anchovies
64, 99, 114, 153, 184

Beef
52, 125, 157

Butter
16, 24, 34, 36, 41, 71, 75, 78, 84, 120, 141, 144,
145, 169, 170, 179, 204, 212, 217, 218, 219, 224,
226, 230, 236, 240

Cheese
16, 24, 48, 54, 71, 81, 84, 91, 99, 114, 120, 122,
128, 136, 141, 143, 150, 154, 158, 166, 179, 199,
200, 232

Chicken
117, 122, 143, 144

Chicken stock
16, 24, 127, 149, 158, 169

Cream
136, 141, 169, 199, 204, 223, 230, 236

Cream cheese
212, 217, 226

Crème fraîche
170, 218, 240

Fish
114, 119, 149, 193

Lamb
144, 157

Milk
24, 41, 106, 136, 141, 163, 179, 218, 226, 230

Pork
110, 131

Prosciutto
184

Ricotta
71, 81, 158, 232

Sausages
131

Yoghurt
38, 41, 42, 48, 68, 72, 75, 78, 105, 110, 145, 154,
163, 165, 193, 195, 217

NUTS & SEEDS

Almonds
145, 236

Cashews
92

Coconut flakes
217, 223

Desiccated coconut
212

Hazelnuts
99

Peanuts
59

Pecans
212, 236

Pine nuts
78, 83, 128, 141, 145, 170

Pistachios
68, 230

Poppy seeds
92

Pumpkin seeds
91, 236

Sesame seeds
44, 54, 165, 193, 236, 240

Walnuts
236

OTK

SHELF LOVE

Noor Murad & Yotam Ottolenghi

Photography by Elena Heatherwick

Contents

Introduction

THE ARCHES

There's a railway arch in north London, built from equal parts brick and tahini, walls coated in olive oil and floors stained with spice: habanero and fenugreek, Aleppo chilli and black lime. To the outsider it is identified through stacks of wooden pallets, blue shutters, red brick and industrial steel, easily missed and effortlessly unglamorous. To the insider, it's a tiny bit more. This is the Ottolenghi Test Kitchen, the OTK to some, where a stripped-back railway arch makes absolute sense, where a group of individuals meet and eat, cook and write, tear and share and gather with just one motive: to create good food with good ingredients, and to share it with the world.

THE TEAM

Those who know us will tell you that Yotam Ottolenghi and his Test Kitchen colleagues are an eccentric bunch, our various backgrounds and stories leading us to this one shared space. To say that the Test Kitchen can be narrowed down to one voice would be inaccurate, really, when it is in fact a collection of voices and personalities, the comings and goings of chefs and writers, of food stylists and photographers, of sommeliers and every other talent in the trade. It is a decade of collected fingerprints, the kind of space you walk into and know, 'This place is greater than the sum of its parts.'

Leading the crew you have Noor Murad, who informally crowns herself the queen of Middle Eastern feasts; Verena Lochmuller, who is basically the Google search engine to all baking questions; Ixta Belfrage, co-author of *Flavour* and our inside scoop to the latest foodie trends; Tara Wigley, the in-house word wizard; and, of course, Gitai Fisher, the man who keeps us all in check while making absolutely sure we stay out of trouble. There's also our trusted colleague Claudine Boulstridge, our secret OTK weapon, who tries and tests all of our recipes from her family kitchen in Wales. The latest addition to our team of misfits is Chaya, who joined just as the book was coming together, adding heaped spoonfuls of spicy personality to the brew. Ultimately, of course, there is Big Y, as we dub him, who pushes and inspires us, while making sure we have enough wiggle room to sail our own course. Our stories are sprinkled across this book, written and narrated by Noor, whose Middle Eastern influence makes a prominent mark on these pages.

THE STORY

The year is 2020. It doesn't need an introduction, more of an acknowledgement, that this is the year in which the rug was pulled out from under the world's feet. Suddenly, and blindly, we found ourselves dispersed and separated, across borders and continents

alike. Unstable ground had us grabbing for what was true and familiar and, to no surprise, all steps led to our kitchens. We did what we all do best, and began creating recipes based on what we had in our store cupboards and fridges, our freezers and pantries. We grabbed and raided and rummaged and emptied. We stripped down our kitchens to build up our tables and soon realised that any recipe – any food, any dish – can be made unequivocally 'Ottolenghi' with the right know-how, the right willingness to work with what you have.

So 2020, the most momentous of all years, brought with it the first OTK cookbook, the one in which we teach you a skill or two that we've recently learned – how to cleverly utilise your kitchen finds while putting a delicious meal on the table. We see it as the first of many stories the Ottolenghi Test Kitchen has to tell, tales of other timely skills that are yet to reveal themselves, accounts of our food adventures and all the little discoveries that we're so desperate to share with you.

THE BOOK

For the longest time, we called this book 'Stripped'; we thought of it as a stripping down of our shelves, pantries, cupboards, fridges and freezers. It felt like a liberation, getting rid of the old to make way for the new. In turn, we wanted to set the foundations and framework in place for you to flex your own creativity, stripping down your own kitchens, raiding your own shelves and swapping things out with your own pantry ingredients. This decluttering approach was freeing, teaching us how to love our kitchens and our stoves, but most importantly teaching us how to love ourselves at an otherwise very challenging time. And so *Shelf Love* (thank you, Caz!), was born, a whimsical description, yes, but also a truly accurate one.

To build up this book we have broken down our kitchens: pulling ingredients apart only to put them back together again – cohesive dishes based on kitchen finds. A bag of dried chickpeas, repurposed. A kilo of onions, cooked down. Some wonky-looking vegetables, chargrilled. There is a 'this for that' ethos here; the understanding that, in this new world, the need to improvise, to roll with the punches, is more crucial than ever before.

We carry this ethos throughout the book, as we map out our recipes based on kitchen logistics: from fridge to pantry to one-dish bakes and sweet, sweet endings. It's food that we'd cook at home, for our friends and families, comforting but with a slight edge, a little twist, a 'cheffy' addition. They're recipes with stories and personalities, with swap-outs and suggestions, recipes that say without saying, 'I'll show you the rules, but here's how to break them.' We want you to take these recipes and make them your own, turning this cookbook into a handbook – one to write and scribble on, to stain with turmeric and fold down pages. We want this book to be *that* book, the most haggard-looking book on your shelves, indicating that it serves its purpose and then some. We want, more than anything, for you to show this book some love. Shelf Love.

THAT ONE SHELF IN THE

BACK OF YOUR PANTRY

That one shelf in the back of your pantry

Sitting on that one shelf in the very back of the pantry, all the way to the right, behind the tins, you'll find a forgotten bag of . . . mung beans? Wholemeal flour? Polenta? The beauty in a shelf is that no two are identical, with each turning up with something different to show. Some of them are tin-heavy, others full of jars or dried legumes, and some filled to the brim with every pasta shape known to man. Perhaps it's knowing that pantry ingredients have a very long shelf-life which means there's no real rush to use them until the inevitable clear-out, the 'I'm so sure I had some couscous around here somewhere' moment. But the day you do finally get round to decluttering is a day filled with infinite opportunities for reinvention.

Some of our favourite pairings at the Test Kitchen have come from a quick brainstorm and a good rummage through our store cupboards: semolina with coconut, black lime with feta, butter beans with preserved lemon. We go in with the mindset that the only limitations in food are the ones we set for ourselves, that rules are meant to be broken and that everything works unless proven otherwise. After that it's a balancing act, finding that happy medium between what we envisage and what we already know. If there's one thing our very interconnected world has taught us it's this: whatever it is, it's probably already been done – the key is to find new ways to speak with food, while still paying tribute to the culture (or cultures) the recipe was inspired by. This often leads to dishes that are familiar, but also not: take tabbouleh and turn it into a fritter (p. 56), eat porridge but make it savoury (p. 36), load a French onion soup with chickpeas and warming spices (p. 16). Sometimes, though, it's all about meeting a dish where it's at, and resisting the urge to re-create it: see creamy dreamy hummus (p. 20).

The premise of this book is built on a shelf raid, as is evident throughout this chapter, but really it moves beyond that. On the one hand, shelf clear-outs lead you to become more resourceful with your meals, while, on the other, they create a blank slate for you to refill and restock. Recent times have been all about that: out with the old and in with the new, stripping it all down to build it back up, removing what once was to introduce what now is. This chapter is dedicated to the 'out', the 'strip' and the 'remove', which in turn creates room to play.

(One jar of) butter beans with preserved lemon, chilli and herb oil

Prep time: *20 minutes*
Cook time: *40 minutes*

Butter beans are given the superstar treatment with this preserved lemon, chilli and herb oil. The longer the beans sit in the oil, the better they become, so feel free to make these the day before, allowing them to become wonderful little sponges overnight. Be sure to use good-quality jarred butter beans here; it'll make all the difference. Serve with crusty bread to mop it all up, and maybe some grilled manouri or halloumi.

Serves 4, as part of a mezze spread

5 garlic cloves, *finely chopped*

2 mild red chillies, *finely chopped, seeds and all (30g)*

1 tbsp coriander seeds, *finely crushed with a pestle and mortar*

3 preserved lemons *(80g), inner parts discarded and skin finely sliced (45g)*

1½ tbsp roughly chopped thyme leaves

4 rosemary sprigs

1 tbsp tomato paste

170ml olive oil

1 jar of butter beans *(700g) (we like the Brindisa brand), drained (550g)*

2 large vine tomatoes *(220g), roughly grated (p. 88) and skins discarded (120g)*

flaked sea salt and black pepper

1. Put the first eight ingredients and 1¼ teaspoons of flaked salt into a medium sauté pan on a medium-low heat and stir everything together. Heat gently for 25 minutes, or until very fragrant but not at all browned. If the oil gets too hot, turn the heat down to low. Stir in the butter beans, then turn the heat up to medium and cook for 10 minutes. Remove from the heat and leave to infuse for at least an hour, or longer if time allows.

2. Meanwhile, mix the grated tomato with ⅓ teaspoon of flaked sea salt and a good grind of pepper.

3. To serve, pour the butter bean mixture into a shallow bowl and spoon over the grated tomato, mixing it in in places.

Make it your own:
– Swap out the butter beans for cannellini beans or chickpeas.

_____

_____

_____

Hawaij onion and chickpea soup with cheesy toast

Prep time: *30 minutes*
Cook time: *1 hour 50 minutes*

This is based on French onion soup. Similar to the classic, a large quantity of onions is cooked low and slow (use a food processor or mandolin to help you slice them), but everything else from that point on is a deviation. Hawaij is a Yemeni spice blend which complements the sweet onions, adding complexity and warmth, and the chickpeas add bulk, making this a meal in a bowl. The cheesy toast is optional but . . . it is melty cheese on crunchy toast after all, and we really think you should make it.

Serves 4, generously

50g unsalted butter

2 tbsp olive oil

1.2kg onions *(about 7–8), halved and thinly sliced*

250g tomato passata

30g fresh coriander, *roughly chopped*

1 tin of chickpeas *(400g), drained (240g)*

1.5 litres chicken or vegetable stock

salt and black pepper

SPICE MIX

1 tbsp coriander seeds

2 tsp cumin seeds

2 whole cloves

8 cardamom pods, *shells discarded and seeds reserved*

½ tsp fenugreek seeds

½ tsp ground turmeric

CHEESY TOAST (OPTIONAL)

220g mature cheddar, *roughly grated*

10g fresh coriander, *roughly chopped*

1 large garlic clove, *crushed*

6 slices of sourdough, *cut about 2cm thick (350g)*

15g unsalted butter, *softened at room temperature*

1 tbsp Dijon mustard

1. Put the butter and oil into a large cast-iron saucepan on a medium-high heat. Once hot, stir in the onions, then turn the heat down to medium and cook, gently, for 1 hour, stirring only every 10 minutes or so. You want the onions to completely soften and turn golden.

2. Meanwhile, make the spice mix. Put the coriander and cumin seeds, cloves, cardamom and fenugreek into a small frying pan and place it on a medium-high heat. Toast for 5 minutes, then blitz in a spice grinder to a smooth powder (or use a pestle and mortar). Stir in the turmeric and set aside.

3. When the onions are ready, turn the heat to medium-high. Add the spice mix, passata and fresh coriander and cook for 5 minutes, stirring occasionally. Add the chickpeas, stock, 1¾ teaspoons of salt and a very generous amount of black pepper and bring to the boil. Turn the heat to medium and simmer, stirring occasionally, for 30 minutes.

4. For the cheesy toast, preheat the oven to its highest grill setting. In a small bowl combine the cheese with the fresh coriander, garlic and a good grind of pepper.

5. When the soup is almost ready, place the bread on a parchment-lined baking tray. Grill for 1 minute, then remove from the oven and flip over. Brush the untoasted side with the softened butter, then the Dijon mustard. Top with the cheese mixture and grill for 3–4 minutes, until golden and bubbly. Cut each slice into three.

6. Divide the soup between four bowls and top with a piece of the cheesy toast, serving any extra cheesy toast alongside.

> *Get ahead:*
> – Make the whole soup the day ahead; the flavours will only intensify over time.

Make it your own:
- Swap out the chickpeas for tinned cannellini beans, black-eyed beans or kidney beans.
- Use any soft herb and a different blend of spices.
- Veganise it: use a vegan cheese, veggie stock, and olive oil in place of butter.

_____

_____

On hummus

Hummus has made its appearance in many an Ottolenghi recipe, and for good reason. It is a universally loved food, so much so that it could practically be its own food group. Recently, Noor wrote a little ode to hummus, sharing her tips, tricks and hummus hacks, and was amazed at the response. What seemed like second nature to her was not always the case for others and, all of a sudden, hummus regained its rightful place on the throne of foods-we-need-to-continue-talking-about.

A little frustrated at the widespread hummus mishaps, Noor took it upon herself to write a detailed step-by-step guide on how to achieve the ultimate creamy dreamy hummus (p.20), using both tinned and dried chickpeas. 'I've come to realise,' she wrote, 'that you're all a bunch of die-hard hummus lovers and this is the only way to your tahini-laden hearts'. Hummus, dear reader, is a science. Go through these tips carefully, pedantic as they may seem, and you will soon be on your way to the creamiest dreamiest hummus that ever did exist.

1. If starting with dried chickpeas, be sure to cook them very well. You want them to be very soft, with no bite. If using tinned, simmer them in fresh water for a good 15–20 minutes after peeling (step 4) – this will soften them further.

2. Use warm chickpeas as these are softer and easier to blend, and are the first step to achieving a smooth hummus with no grit.

3. Salt your chickpea water towards the last 15 minutes of cooking time. Also add a pinch of ground cumin to the water, which will give a subtle cumin flavour to your hummus. Save the cooking water. You can use it as a base for soups and stews but, more importantly, you'll be using this flavourful cumin-chickpea water to thin out your hummus.

4. Peel your chickpeas (i.e. remove the skins). We know it is a bit of an ask, but it really does make a difference. The chickpeas need to be agitated and there are two ways to do this. Either agitate your cooked chickpeas in their hot water, releasing the skins and using a sieve to scoop and discard those that rise to the surface. Alternatively, and this works best with tinned chickpeas, spread them out between two tea towels and rub them together, without crushing them. The friction will release the skins, allowing you to easily pick them out and discard them.

5. Add a couple of ice cubes to the food processor when blending your hummus. The cold shock of ice against the warm chickpeas will aerate your hummus to wonderful heights.

6. Resist the temptation to add olive oil to the base of your hummus. There's plenty of fat in the tahini to give you a beautifully homogenised hummus mixture. Adding olive oil will simply mess with the holy matrimony of chickpea and sesame paste, which you really don't want. Do, however, pour a generous amount of good-quality olive oil on top of the hummus once you've plated it.

7. Source the best-quality tahini you can find. We highly recommend tahini made from hulled sesame seeds and light in colour, and typically made in the Levant region in countries such as Lebanon or Palestine. Avoid unhulled 'sesame pastes' that are dark and gritty. We can't stress enough how important it is to seek out authentic tahini; it really will make or break your hummus. The key to creamy dreamy is in the tahini, really.

Dried vs tinned:
In the brave battle of dried vs tinned, dried chickpeas won the OTK hummus wars, earning the crown for the creamiest dreamiest hummus, and the hearts of the whole team. It is worth noting, however, that not everyone has the luxury of time to soak dried chickpeas, and we firmly believe that you *can* achieve a close runner-up using tinned chickpeas . . . provided you follow our tips and tricks.

Creamy dreamy hummus

Prep time: *10 minutes*
Cook time: *40–90 minutes*
Soaking time (if dried):
overnight

This basic hummus recipe follows the tips and tricks referenced on pp. 18–19. Serve this alongside the pillowy pitas on p. 23.

Serves 6, as part of a mezze spread

200g dried chickpeas,
 soaked overnight in plenty of water and ¾ tsp bicarbonate of soda
or
2 tins of chickpeas *(800g),*
 drained (480g)
½ tsp bicarbonate of soda
 (if using dried)
1 pinch ground cumin
120–150g tahini
1 garlic clove, *crushed,*
 or more to taste
1½ tbsp lemon juice,
 or more to taste
salt

YOUR CHOICE OF TOPPINGS
olive oil
any chopped herbs
toasted nuts
rose harissa *or your choice of chilli paste*

1. If using dried chickpeas, drain them well after soaking, then put them into a medium saucepan, for which you have a lid, with the ½ tsp bicarbonate of soda and enough water to cover by about 4cm. Bring to a simmer on a medium-high heat, skimming the scum from the surface as needed, then turn the heat down to medium-low, cover with the lid and simmer from anywhere between 30 and 50 minutes. This will differ greatly depending on your chickpeas, so check them at the 20-minute mark. Towards the last 15 minutes of cooking time, salt the water nicely and add the cumin. Cook your chickpeas until they are very soft.

2. Using a slotted spoon or spider, agitate your chickpeas, giving them a gentle shake in the water, allowing the skins to be released and rise to the surface. Discard the skins (don't worry too much if you don't catch them all). Skip to step 5.

3. If using tinned chickpeas, spread them out between two tea towels and use your hands to vigorously rub the towels together for a few minutes. Don't press down too hard on the chickpeas; you don't want to crush them. Lift the top towel, to see how you're doing – the friction should have caused the chickpea skins to be released. Discard the skins.

4. Put the tinned (and now peeled) chickpeas into a saucepan with enough water to cover, 1 teaspoon of salt and a pinch of cumin. Simmer for 15 minutes, until soft.

5. Drain the chickpeas over a bowl, saving the water. Put the warm chickpeas into a food processor with 120g of tahini, the garlic, lemon juice, a couple of ice cubes (25g worth), 2 tablespoons of reserved chickpea water and a good pinch of salt. Blitz until smooth(ish), then check on your hummus. You might need more tahini, garlic, lemon and salt and very likely more chickpea water. Add a bit of each as you need. Don't be shy about adding more tahini – each brand differs and may require you to use more. Blitz the hummus until very smooth, a few minutes at least. Don't worry about the hummus being too loose; it will thicken as it sits.

6. When ready, spread the hummus in a shallow bowl, creating a well in the centre. (If not serving right away, store in a sealed container in the fridge for up to 2 days.) Top with a generous glug of olive oil, then personalise your hummus as you wish. We sometimes add herbs, toasted nuts or rose harissa, but these are just suggestions. Once you get the base right, hummus knows no bounds.

Tinned Chickpeas

Dried Chickpeas

Dried Chickpeas

Tinned Chickpeas

Pita

Prep time: *5 minutes*
Cook time: *40 minutes*
Proving time: *1 hour*
20 minutes to overnight

Up your pita game by making your own: these pitas are light, airy and pillowy and are the perfect spongy vehicles to stuff, tear, mop and scoop – making the whole eating experience really very satisfying.

Makes 6 pitas

240ml lukewarm water
2 tsp fast-action dried yeast
2 tsp caster sugar
300g plain flour, *plus extra for dusting*
50g wholemeal flour
1 tsp salt
1 tbsp olive oil, *plus extra for oiling*

1. Put the water into a small bowl and sprinkle over the yeast and sugar. Leave for 5–6 minutes to react and become foamy.

2. Put both flours and the salt into the bowl of a stand mixer, with the dough hook in place, and mix on low speed to combine. Add the olive oil and the yeast mixture, turning the speed to medium-high, and knead for 7 minutes. The dough should be smooth, elastic and a bit sticky.

3. Transfer the dough to a well-oiled large bowl, cover with a damp tea towel and leave to rise in a warm place for 1–2 hours, or until doubled in size. Alternatively, leave to prove, covered and refrigerated, overnight.

4. Transfer the dough to a lightly floured work surface and divide into six 100g pieces. Use your hands to roll each piece into a round ball. Cover with a damp tea towel and leave to rest for 20 minutes.

5. Preheat the oven to 240°C fan or your highest oven setting. Place a large baking tray in the oven to warm up.

6. Cut out two pieces of baking parchment roughly the size of your baking tray, lay them out on your work surface and sprinkle them with a little flour. Top one piece of paper with two balls of dough, spaced well apart, and use a lightly floured rolling pin to roll each one out into a round, roughly 12cm in diameter. Don't tear or overwork the pitas at all, or they won't puff up.

7. Carefully transfer the paper with the two rolled-out rounds to your preheated tray and bake for 4–5 minutes, or until lightly golden and puffy. Transfer to a clean bowl and cover with a damp tea towel to keep warm (save the parchment paper to reuse again). While they're in the oven, prepare the other two rounds in the same way and, when ready, transfer them to the hot tray and bake in the same way. Continue until you've made six pitas in total. Keep them covered in the bowl until you're ready to serve.

Get ahead:
- Make the dough the night before, leaving it to prove in the fridge overnight and bringing it back up to room temperature when you're ready to work with it again.
- Freeze the raw dough once you've rolled it into rounds, wrapping it very well before storing it in an airtight container. Defrost before cooking.

Cheesy polenta and tomato sauce

Prep time: *20 minutes*
Cook time: *45 minutes*

This is polenta dressed to impress as a veggie main, but not so overdressed that it can't also work as a side dish, such as to roast chicken or grilled fish. Don't make the polenta until just before you're about to serve, as you don't want it to be completely set.

Serves 4

500ml vegetable stock, *or chicken stock, if not veggie*
350ml whole milk
60g unsalted butter
200g quick-cook polenta
150g Gruyère, *roughly grated*

TOMATO SAUCE
150g datterini or regular cherry tomatoes
90ml olive oil
1 onion, *peeled and cut into 8 wedges (150g)*
6 garlic cloves, *crushed*
750g vine tomatoes, *cored and finely chopped into 1cm cubes (seeds and all)*
1 tsp caster sugar
5g oregano sprigs, *plus 1½ tbsp picked leaves*
salt and black pepper

1. Place a large sauté pan on a high heat and, once very hot, add the datterini/cherry tomatoes and char for 5 minutes. Remove from the pan and set aside, then let the pan cool slightly.

2. Return the pan to a medium-high heat along with 4 tablespoons of oil and the onion. Cook for 12 minutes, stirring occasionally, until softened and golden, then add the garlic and cook for 30 seconds more. Add the chopped vine tomatoes, sugar, picked oregano leaves, 100ml of water, 1 teaspoon of salt and plenty of pepper and bring to the boil. Lower the heat to medium and cook for 20 minutes, stirring every now and then, until the tomatoes have started to break down. Add the charred datterini tomatoes and cook for 8 minutes more, until the sauce has thickened. Keep warm on a low heat.

3. Heat the remaining 2 tablespoons of oil in a small frying pan on a medium-high heat. Add the oregano sprigs and cook for just 60 seconds, or until the leaves start to turn a deep green. Set aside.

4. Meanwhile, put the stock, milk, 100ml of water, half the butter, 1¼ teaspoons of salt and a good grind of pepper into a medium saucepan on a medium-high heat. Bring to a gentle simmer, then turn the heat to medium-low and slowly add the polenta, whisking continuously, until completely incorporated. Continue whisking for 2–3 minutes, until the polenta is cooked and the mixture is quite wet. Stir through the cheese and the remaining butter. Remove from the heat.

5. Spread the polenta out on a large platter. Spoon the tomato sauce on top, gently swirling some into the polenta. Top with the fried oregano and its oil, and serve warm.

Get ahead:
– Make the sauce up to 2 days ahead, warming it through to serve.

Make it your own:
– Play around with different cheeses, herbs and spices.

_____

_____

Make it your own:
- Play with your beans – we love this with chickpeas too.
- Play with your herbs – use what you have on hand.

_____

_____

Green cannellini and tahini

Prep time: *25 minutes*
Cook time: *40 minutes*

Variations of warm beans served with tahini are popular throughout the Arab world, with dishes such as chickpea fatteh and ful mudammas with tahini at the forefront. Such dishes are typically eaten warm for breakfast, and are a sure way to keep you full until dinner. They're the inspiration for these herby cannellini beans, which can easily be served at any mealtime.

Serves 4 as a main, or 6 as a side

1 round white or brown pita *(100g), pocket opened up, then roughly torn into 2–3cm pieces (see p. 23 for homemade pita)*

1 tbsp za'atar

75ml olive oil

3 tins of cannellini beans *(1.2kg), drained (720g)*

30g parsley, *roughly chopped*

30g fresh coriander, *roughly chopped*

30g chives, *roughly chopped*

1¼ tsp cumin seeds, *toasted and roughly crushed with a pestle and mortar*

1 garlic clove, *crushed*

2½ tbsp lemon juice

salt and black pepper

TAHINI SAUCE

80g tahini

1½ tbsp lemon juice

1 garlic clove, *crushed*

CHILLI OIL

2½ tbsp olive oil

½ tsp chilli flakes

¼ tsp paprika

1. Preheat the oven to 180°C fan. Toss the pita with the za'atar, 2 tablespoons of oil, ¼ teaspoon of salt and a good grind of pepper, and spread out on a medium, parchment-lined baking tray. Bake for 12 minutes, tossing halfway, or until golden and crispy. Set aside to cool.

2. Set aside 100g of the beans in a medium bowl. Put the remaining beans, 600ml of water and 1 teaspoon of salt into a medium saucepan on a medium-high heat. Bring to the boil, then simmer for 15 minutes, or until the beans are nicely softened and warmed through. Keep warm on a low heat until ready to serve.

3. Make the tahini sauce by whisking together all the ingredients with 70ml of water and ¼ teaspoon of salt in a medium bowl, until smooth and pourable. It will thicken as it sits.

4. Make the chilli oil by putting the oil and chilli flakes into a small frying pan and placing it on a medium heat. Cook for 4 minutes, then add the paprika and remove the pan from the heat. Set aside.

5. Put the reserved 100g of beans into a food processor, along with the herbs, cumin, garlic, lemon juice, the remaining 3 tablespoons of oil, ⅛ teaspoon of salt and a good grind of pepper. Blitz until smooth, then transfer to a large mixing bowl.

6. Drain the warm beans in a sieve set over a bowl, then add them and 100ml of their cooking liquid to the herb mixture, mixing well to combine. You want the beans to be well coated and for the whole mixture to be saucy (but not overly wet), so add a couple of tablespoons more of the cooking liquid if you wish (discarding the remainder).

7. Transfer to a large, lipped platter and drizzle over half the tahini sauce and all the chilli oil. Sprinkle with half the pita and serve warm, with the extra tahini and pita alongside.

Za'atar parathas with grated tomato

Prep time: *10 minutes*
Cook time: *1 hour*
Resting time: *20 minutes*

Parathas are flaky South Asian flatbreads – these particular ones are based on Indian laccha paratha, which uses semolina in the dough. There's a bit of a knack to making them but once you get the hang of the process, they are not complicated. Cutting the dough, as we do here, is actually a really simple way of achieving those flaky paratha layers and, once you've mastered the method, they're also quite fun to make! Traditionally there'd be some ghee involved, but we've kept these vegan and also included za'atar and grated tomato, Noor's sneaky additions. Serve these as part of a brunch spread or as a snack.

Makes 6 parathas

270g plain flour
40g semolina
1 tsp salt
1 tsp caster sugar
75ml olive oil
140–160ml lukewarm water
3 tbsp za'atar
4 tbsp sunflower oil, *plus extra for greasing/oiling*

GRATED TOMATO
320g vine tomatoes (about 3)
1 garlic clove, *crushed*
2 tbsp olive oil
salt and black pepper

1. Put the flour, semolina, salt and sugar into a large bowl and use your fingers to mix everything together. Add 1 tablespoon of the olive oil, using your hands to incorporate, then slowly start to pour in the water, using your free hand to bring the dough together into a shaggy mass. Use about 120ml of water at first and then slowly add more; you'll use about 155ml in total, give or take. Add a little more if you think it needs it. The mixture will seem quite wet at first but this is how it should be.

2. Transfer to a clean work surface and knead for 5 minutes, until you have a smooth, pliable dough that isn't at all sticky. Transfer it to a lightly oiled bowl, cover with a damp tea towel and leave to rest for 20 minutes.

3. Meanwhile, use a box grater to roughly grate the tomatoes (see p. 88), discarding the skins. Transfer the grated tomato to a sieve and leave to drain for about 5 minutes. Put the drained pulp (about 220g) into a bowl with the garlic, oil, ¼ teaspoon of salt and a good grind of pepper. Set aside until needed.

4. Mix together the za'atar and the remaining 4 tablespoons of olive oil in a small bowl.

5. Transfer the dough to a well-oiled surface and divide the mixture into six 80g balls.

6. Working with one piece at a time, and keeping the rest under a damp tea towel, use a well-greased rolling pin to roll out the dough as thin as it can go without tearing, about 1mm thick and 30cm in diameter (it'll start to look a little transparent). Don't worry if it's not a perfect circle: it doesn't need to be.

7. Using a small sharp knife, cut the dough lengthways into multiple 1cm-wide strips.

8. Drizzle about a tablespoon of the za'atar oil all over the strips, using your hands or the back of a spoon to gently spread it all over the surface.

9. Use your fingers to push the strips together so that you end up with one long piece of dough.

10. Then, using your dominant hand, wind the whole thing around the four fingers of your other hand and tuck the end through the centre, to form a round. It will look like a bird's nest. Continue in this way with the remaining dough, making sure your work surface is well oiled each time.

11. Roll out each of the rounds into a 10–12cm disc.

12. In a medium frying pan on a medium heat, cook each paratha for 3 minutes on each side. Brush the top with about 1 teaspoon of sunflower oil, then flip over, cook for another minute, brushing the other side with another teaspoon of oil, flipping again and cooking for a final minute. Place the cooked paratha on a tray or plate and cover with a tea towel (this'll help keep it nice and soft). Continue in this way with the rest, using two pans to speed things up.

13. Serve the parathas with the grated tomato alongside.

Make it your own:

– Play around with different spices, or make these parathas plain with some ghee instead of the za'atar oil, if you're not vegan.

_____

_____

_____

Chaat masala chickpea and polenta chips

Prep time: *15 minutes*
Cook time: *45 minutes*
Setting time: *30 minutes*

These chips celebrate our favourite little bean in its multiple forms by using chickpea (gram) flour for the base, and then whole chickpeas and chickpea water (aquafaba) for a wonderfully vegan mayo. We love the sour tang you get from the chaat masala here, thanks to the mango powder in this Indian spice mix.

Serves 4, as a snack

1 small red onion, *finely chopped (90g)*
1 tbsp lemon juice
2¼ tsp chaat masala
⅓ tsp ground turmeric
3½ tbsp olive oil
100g gram flour
100g quick-cook polenta
10g fresh coriander, *roughly chopped*
2 green chillies, *finely chopped, deseeded if you don't like heat*
salt and black pepper

CHICKPEA MAYO
1 tin of chickpeas *(400g)*
1 garlic clove, *crushed*
½ tbsp English mustard *(we use Colman's)*
½ tbsp lemon juice
150ml sunflower oil

1. Put the onion, lemon juice and ¼ teaspoon of salt into a small bowl and set aside to pickle and soften.

2. Line a 24cm x 18cm baking dish with a piece of baking parchment large enough to cover the bottom and sides.

3. Put 2 teaspoons of the chaat masala, all the turmeric, 2 tablespoons of olive oil, 700ml of water, 1 teaspoon of salt and a good grind of pepper into a medium saucepan on a medium-high heat. Bring to a simmer, then turn the heat to low. Combine the gram flour and polenta together in a bowl and stir until well combined. Slowly pour this into the seasoned water, whisking continuously to ensure there are no big lumps (there'll still be a few small ones). Cook for 4 minutes, whisking vigorously, until the mixture has thickened and starts to pull away from the sides of the pan. Quickly transfer the mixture to your prepared tin, smoothing out the top with a spatula. Set aside to cool, about 10 minutes, then cover and refrigerate to set for 30 minutes.

4. Make the mayo. Drain the tin of chickpeas over a bowl. Measure out 50g of the chickpeas (save the rest for another recipe)

and 40ml of the chickpea water (discard the rest). Put the chickpea water, measured-out chickpeas, garlic, mustard, lemon juice and ⅛ teaspoon of salt into a food processor and blitz until smooth, scraping the sides as you go along. With the motor running, very slowly drizzle in the sunflower oil, until the mixture comes together into a loose mayonnaise-like consistency. Transfer to a small bowl (refrigerate if getting ahead).

5. Preheat the oven to 220°C fan. Transfer the chickpea-polenta mixture from the tin and on to a cutting board. Trim the edges to give you a neat rectangle, then cut lengthways into 12 slices and then widthways in half, to get 24 pieces in total.

6. Spread the chickpea chips out on to a large parchment-lined baking tray. Drizzle all over with the remaining 1½ tablespoons of olive oil and bake for 25 minutes, turning halfway, until golden and crisp. Pile on to a plate and sprinkle with the remaining ¼ teaspoon of chaat masala and a little salt.

7. Stir the coriander and chillies into the bowl with the pickled onion and serve this and the mayo alongside.

Make it your own:

- If you can't find chaat masala, then mild curry powder works well here too!
- Serve with plain yoghurt or store-bought mayo if you like, for non-vegans.

_____

_____

Yellow split pea purée with buttered onions and caper salsa

Prep time: *15 minutes*
Cook time: *1 hour 30 minutes*

Yotam's love affair with the Mediterranean means those signature staples – fatty olive oil, salty feta, briny capers! – permeate both his home kitchen and the OTK. This purée is a take on fava, a Greek mezze dish of yellow split peas with capers and red onion. It's fantastic served as a dip, but also works alongside grilled fish or roasted meat.

Serves 6 as a dip, or 4 as a side

3 tbsp unsalted butter

3 tbsp olive oil

2 red onions, *finely chopped*

180g yellow split peas,
  rinsed well and drained

½ tsp ground turmeric

salt

CAPER SALSA

2 tbsp capers, *roughly chopped*

5g parsley, *finely chopped*

2 thin lemon slices, *pips discarded and the slices finely chopped (flesh, rind and all)*

2 tbsp olive oil

1. Put the butter, 2 tablespoons of oil, the onions and ¾ teaspoon of salt into a large sauté pan, for which you have a lid, on a medium heat, and cook for 15–18 minutes, stirring often, until soft and deeply golden. Transfer half the onions, along with most of the oil and melted butter, to a small bowl and set aside, to serve.

2. Add the split peas, turmeric, 1.2 litres of water and ¾ teaspoon of salt to the pan with the remaining onions and bring to a simmer on a medium-high heat. Lower the heat to medium and cook for 20 minutes, uncovered. Cover with the lid and cook for another 40–45 minutes, or until the split peas are very soft and most of the liquid has evaporated.

3. Meanwhile, combine all the ingredients for the caper salsa together in a small bowl.

4. While the split peas are still warm, put them, together with any remaining cooking water and the last tablespoon of oil, into a food processor and blitz until completely smooth.

5. Spoon into a shallow dish, creating a dip in the middle. Mix the buttered onions with the caper salsa, then spoon on to the dip. Serve warm, or at room temperature.

Make it your own:
– Veganise it: swap the butter for olive oil.

_____

_____

_____

Savoury oat porridge with ginger-garlic crumbs

Prep time: *10 minutes*
Cook time: *35 minutes*

Breakfasts are a solo affair at the OTK, with each person left to their own devices. Tara with her big ol' bowl of eggs and greens, Ixta and Noor with their 'every green' green smoothies, and Gitai with his one-cup-of-coffee-in-silence, please. Verena will, more times than not, rustle up a bowl of porridge, sweet spices and raisins stirred through, warm and inviting and easy on the tummy.

This porridge gets a savoury twist, thanks to the addition of an umami-rich soy butter and crispy ginger-garlic yumbits. Feel free to quadruple the amount of said yumbits: they're so good sprinkled on to eggs, rice and every other food group (we think).

Serves 4, for breakfast or brunch

12 spring onions, *trimmed and halved lengthways* (180g)

3 tbsp olive oil

80g fresh ginger, *peeled and finely grated*

12 garlic cloves (*about 1 head*), *crushed*

4 large eggs

160g jumbo rolled oats (*gluten-free if you wish*)

2 tbsp soy sauce

50g unsalted butter, *fridge cold and cut into 2cm cubes*

1 tsp chilli flakes, *or more if you like extra heat*

salt and black pepper

1. Toss the spring onions in a bowl with 1 tablespoon of oil and a pinch each of salt and pepper. Place a large, non-stick sauté pan on a high heat and, once hot, cook half the spring onions for 3 minutes, turning a couple of times, until softened and charred. Transfer to a plate and char the remaining half, adding to the plate when done. Let the pan cool slightly.

2. Wipe out the pan and place it on a medium heat with the remaining 2 tablespoons of oil. Once hot, add the ginger and garlic and cook for 15 minutes, stirring occasionally, until deeply golden and crispy. Transfer two-thirds of this mixture to a small bowl and leave the rest in the pan.

3. Meanwhile, boil the eggs for 6 minutes, until soft-boiled (or longer if preferred). Drain, peel and set aside.

4. To the ginger-garlic pan add the oats, 1 litre of water, 1 teaspoon of salt and a good grind of pepper. Bring to a gentle simmer on a medium-high heat, then cook for about 4 minutes, stirring occasionally, until you have a loose porridge. Add a splash more water if needed.

5. Meanwhile, put the soy sauce and a generous amount of pepper into a small saucepan and bring to a simmer on a medium-high heat. Turn the heat down to low and slowly whisk in the butter cubes, 2–3 at a time, waiting until just melted before adding some more. Continue in this way until you have a homogenised mixture. Don't let it boil at all as it will split.

6. Divide the porridge between four bowls. Top each with some of the soy butter and spring onions. Cut the eggs in half, sprinkle with salt and pepper and place on top. Finish with the reserved ginger-garlic crumbs and a sprinkling of chilli flakes. Serve warm.

Make it your own:

– Skip the charred spring onions and just add some fresh herbs.
– Bulk out your porridge by topping with leftover cooked veggies.
– Make it gluten-free by swapping out the soy with tamari or
  coconut aminos.

_____

_____

Tamarind, greens and mung beans with turmeric oil

Prep time: *30 minutes*
Cook time: *1 hour 20 minutes*
Soaking time: *1 hour +*

Thanks to Bahera Agahi for the inspiration for this dish, a lady well versed in the art of Persian cooking. When asked for a recipe, Bahera chuckled and said, 'I measure by hand and cook by eye and this is how a dish is made.' Noor watched Bahera cook that day, with a mental note to bring this dish to life at the test kitchen. Serve with fluffy white rice, for a complete meal.

Serves 4

105ml olive oil

2 large onions, *thinly sliced (420g)*

10 garlic cloves, *5 crushed and 5 thinly sliced*

2 green chillies, *finely chopped, seeds and all (25g)*

2 tsp cumin seeds, *roughly crushed with a pestle and mortar*

1 tsp mild curry powder

1 tbsp tomato paste

120g dried green mung beans, *soaked in plenty of cold water for at least 1 hour, then drained*

1kg Swiss chard, *stalks reserved for another use and leaves roughly shredded (480g)*

1 tsp caster sugar

3 tbsp tamarind paste

40g fresh coriander, *roughly chopped, plus a handful of extra picked leaves to serve*

½ tsp ground turmeric

½ tsp chilli flakes *(optional)*

½ lemon

130g Greek-style yoghurt

salt and black pepper

1. Heat 4 tablespoons of oil in a large sauté pan, for which you have a lid, on a medium-high heat. Add the onions and cook for 15–18 minutes, stirring occasionally, until softened and deeply browned. Transfer a third of the onions to a bowl and set aside. To the pan, add the crushed garlic, chillies, spices and tomato paste and cook for another minute. Add the drained mung beans and 800ml of water and bring to the boil. Turn the heat down to medium, cover with the lid and leave to simmer gently, stirring occasionally, for about 30–35 minutes, or until the mung beans have softened but still retain their shape.

2. Add the Swiss chard, sugar, 1 teaspoon of salt and a good grind of pepper, then replace the lid and cook for another 10 minutes. Remove the lid and cook for 10 minutes more, or until the chard has softened and the liquid has thickened. Stir in the tamarind and coriander and keep warm until ready to serve.

3. Towards the last 10 minutes of cooking, put the remaining 3 tablespoons of oil and the sliced garlic into a small frying pan and place it on a medium heat. Cook, stirring occasionally, until the garlic is lightly golden, about 12 minutes. Add the turmeric and chilli flakes, if using, and remove from the heat.

4. Transfer the mung bean mixture to a large shallow bowl and squeeze over the lemon half. Top with spoonfuls of the yoghurt, followed by the reserved onions, then spoon over the crispy garlic and its oil. Lastly, garnish with the handful of coriander leaves and serve warm.

Make it your own:

– Swap out the chard for spinach or other leafy greens.
– Veganise it: leave out the yoghurt or use a non-dairy
  alternative.

_____

_____

Soda bread with figs, star anise and orange

Prep time: *15 minutes*
Cook time: *1 hour*
Cooling time: *45 minutes*

One loaf, no yeast, no fuss, no proofing time; everyone needs a foolproof soda bread recipe in their repertoire. We've taken a bit of a sweet approach here, marrying figs together with sweet star anise and cinnamon. To balance this out, serve with softened and nicely salted butter and some bitter marmalade if you like.

Serves 6

180ml whole milk
240g Greek-style yoghurt
1 large egg
1 tbsp orange zest
515g plain flour, *plus extra for shaping*
2 tsp ground star anise
1 tsp ground cinnamon
40g caster sugar
1 tsp bicarbonate of soda
½ tsp baking powder
1 tsp salt
70g unsalted butter, *fridge cold and cut into 1½cm cubes*
150g soft dried figs, *cut into 1cm cubes*

1. Preheat the oven to 180°C fan. Line a medium baking tray with baking parchment.

2. Whisk together the milk, yoghurt, egg and orange zest in a medium bowl and set aside.

3. In a separate large bowl, mix together the flour, spices, sugar, bicarbonate of soda, baking powder and salt. Use your hands to rub in the butter until it resembles coarse crumbs similar to large couscous, then stir in the figs. Add the yoghurt mixture and stir to gently combine; do not overmix it – you just want the ingredients to come together (it will be very sticky).

4. Using lightly floured hands, transfer the dough to your prepared tray and shape it into a rough, circular mound similar to a loaf of sourdough, about 18cm in diameter. Use a sharp knife to gently score an 'X' across the top (don't worry if it's not perfect). Bake for 45 minutes, until nicely browned and a skewer inserted into the centre comes out just clean. Transfer to a wire rack to cool, about 45 minutes, before serving.

Make it your own:
– Use other dried fruits and spices (apricot and cardamom would be lovely!).

_____

_____

_____

Yoghurt rice with chana dal and curry leaf oil

Prep time: *20 minutes*
Cook time: *1 hour 5 minutes*
Soaking time: *2 hours to overnight*

This take on Indian 'curd rice' is all at once creamy, hearty, spicy and comforting. We added egg yolk to the base, an untraditional twist, but it makes it a little more velvety and rich. Eliminate this if you like.

Serves 4

100g chana dal, *soaked in plenty of cold water for at least 2 hours (or overnight)*
200g basmati rice, *washed until the water runs clear and drained well*
135ml olive oil
1 large egg yolk
200g Greek-style yoghurt
1 large onion, *finely chopped*
6 garlic cloves, *crushed*
30g fresh ginger, *peeled and finely grated*
2 green chillies, *1 finely chopped and the other thinly sliced, deseeded if you don't like heat*
1 tsp garam masala
3 dried red chillies *(the mild, finger-length variety)*
20 fresh curry leaves *(from 2 sprigs)*
1 tsp black mustard seeds
¼ tsp ground turmeric
salt and black pepper

1. Drain the chana dal, then transfer to a small saucepan with enough water to cover by about 3cm. Bring to the boil on a medium-high heat and simmer for 15–30 minutes, until the dal is cooked but still holds its shape. Timings vary depending on soaking time, so test it at the 15-minute mark (adding more time as needed). Drain in a sieve and run under cold water to stop further cooking.

2. Bring 1.3 litres of water to the boil in a large saucepan. Keep warm on a low heat.

3. Put the rice, 2 tablespoons of oil, 200ml of the hot water and 1¾ teaspoons of salt into a large sauté pan on a medium-high heat. Bring to a simmer, stirring often, until most of the water has been absorbed. Continue in this way, adding 200ml of the hot water at a time and stirring often, until you have used up 1.2 litres of water and the rice resembles a loose, creamy porridge (it will be overcooked), about 20 minutes.

4. Use the back of a spoon to lightly crush the rice grains – you don't want to mash them completely – then turn the heat down to medium-low.

5. Whisk the egg yolk, yoghurt and 50ml of the remaining warm water together in a bowl until smooth.

Add this to the rice, stirring often, and cook for 7 minutes – until thickened slightly, but still a loose porridge. Thin out with more warm water if needed; it tends to thicken as it sits.

6. Meanwhile, make the topping. Heat 3 tablespoons of oil in a large frying pan on a medium-high heat. Add the onion and cook for 8 minutes, stirring occasionally, until browned. Then add the garlic, ginger and chopped green chilli and cook for 4 minutes more. Stir in the chana dal, garam masala, 60ml of water, ¾ teaspoon of salt and a good grind of pepper, and cook, stirring occasionally, until the chana dal starts to brown in places, about 10 minutes. Transfer to a bowl, and cover to keep warm.

7. Wipe out the pan and return it to a medium-high heat. Add the remaining 4 tablespoons of oil and the dried red and sliced green chillies and cook for 3 minutes, until starting to soften but not colour. Add the curry leaves and cook for another 45 seconds, until translucent. Stir in the mustard seeds and turmeric and remove from the heat.

8. To serve, divide the yoghurt rice between four bowls and top with the chana dal mixture. Spoon over the curry leaf oil and its solids and serve warm.

Get ahead:

– Make the rice in advance if you like, but thin it out with a little water when reheating.

Make it your own:
- Eliminate the chilli to make it kid-friendly.
- Swap out the chana dal for other pulses or some roasted vegetablcs.

_____

_____

Ixta's biang biang noodles

Prep time: *10 minutes*
Cook time: *1 hour*
Resting time: *2 hours 30 minutes +*
Cooling time: *1 hour +*

This recipe is inspired by Xi'an Impression, one of Ixta's favourite restaurants in north London, serving the food of the Shanxi Province in China. Determined to learn the art of noodle making, Ixta made this dish during the early days of the first lockdown, showing everyone how to bang bang their biang biang noodles via Instagram. The surge in videos of people making their own were a treat to watch, another way in which food brought the corners of the world together.

It's important to use a plain flour with 10–12% protein – any less than 10% and the dough will rip, rather than stretch. You can find the protein amount in the nutrition information on the side of the packet. Don't worry too much if the noodles rip at the ends – boil them anyway because they will still taste great with the sauces. The technique takes practice and you'll get better as you make them.

Serves 2

NOODLES

300g plain flour *(10–12% protein), sifted*

salt

NUMBING OIL

150ml sunflower oil, *plus extra for greasing*

1 shallot, *finely chopped (60g)*

2 garlic cloves, *finely chopped*

10g fresh ginger, *peeled and finely grated*

½ red chilli, *finely chopped, seeds and all*

1 whole star anise

1 tbsp red bell pepper flakes

1 tsp chilli flakes

1½ tsp Szechuan peppercorns, *roughly crushed*

1½ tsp tomato paste

1 tsp black sesame seeds

1 tsp white sesame seeds

1. For the noodles, mix together the flour and ½ teaspoon of salt in a bowl. Very slowly pour in 150ml of water, stirring with a chopstick. It will look a bit dry – don't be tempted to add more water.

2. Transfer to a greased work surface and use your arm muscles to knead the dough for 5 minutes (it will be quite tough) until it comes together into a shaggy ball. Cover with a damp tea towel and leave to rest for 10 minutes.

3. Knead again vigorously for 10 minutes until the dough is very smooth. It should have the texture of Play-Doh. If you poke it, the indentations should remain, not spring back. Cover with a damp tea towel and leave to rest for another 10 minutes.

4. Cut the dough into eight equal pieces, then roll each piece into a sausage and place it on a well-greased baking tray. Cover well with a damp tea towel and leave to rest at room temperature for 2–3 hours.

5. For the numbing oil, heat 2 tablespoons of oil in a small saucepan on a medium-high heat. Add the next eight ingredients and ¼ teaspoon of salt. Turn the heat down to medium and fry very gently for 5 minutes, stirring often, until the shallot is soft. Add the tomato paste and all the sesame seeds and cook for another 2 minutes. Stir in the remaining 120ml of oil, then reduce the heat to low and cook gently for 20 minutes. If the oil starts to bubble at all, take it off the heat for a minute. Leave to cool and infuse for at least an hour.

6. For the tahini-soy sauce, mix all the ingredients together with a tablespoon of water in a bowl until smooth.

7. Prepare two individual bowls with a large spoonful each of the numbing oil and the tahini-soy sauce. Bring a large pot of water to the boil.

TAHINI-SOY SAUCE

60g tahini (*mix very well before using, to combine the solids and oil*)

2 tbsp soy sauce, *plus extra to serve*

1½ tbsp maple syrup

1½ tbsp rice vinegar

TO SERVE

2 spring onions, *julienned*

1½ tbsp white sesame seeds, *toasted*

8. When ready, roll each piece of dough into a rectangle. Grease your work surface well, then, working with one sausage at a time, use a rolling pin to roll it into a rectangle measuring 16cm x 8cm. Use a chopstick to indent a line lengthways across the middle of the rectangle – this will be your ripping line. Continue with all the sausages in the same way. Leave to rest for 10 minutes.

9. Working with one rectangle at a time, take a shorter end in each hand and start to pull the rectangle slowly and gently until you feel there is no more tension left. Bang the noodle on your work surface about five times, gently stretching the noodle as you go.

10. Using the indent you made earlier, tear the noodle in half lengthways, but not completely, to form a large closed loop. Drop straight into the pan of boiling water, then immediately continue pulling the remaining noodles and adding them to the water. Cook for 1 minute, or until they float to the top.

11. Drain the noodles well, then divide between your prepared bowls.

12. Use chopsticks to mix the noodles together with the oil and sauce, adding more to taste. Top with the spring onions, sesame seeds and a drizzle of soy sauce.

Make it your own:

– We love these sauces so much, so if you don't have time to make your own noodles we urge you to try them using your choice of store-bought noodles!

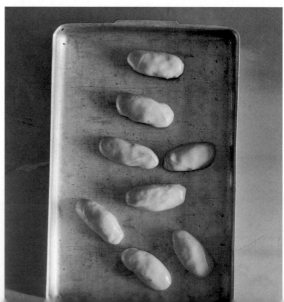

Very giant giant couscous cake

Prep time: *20 minutes*
Cook time: *1 hour 20 minutes*

This very giant cake is very versatile in that you can use other leftover cooked grains or whatever herbs, cheeses and spices you have on hand. Once you've got all your components at the ready, it's a matter of pressing it into the pan and letting it crisp up before the ultimate cake flip. There are two key ways to ensure cake-flip success here: 1) a non-stick pan; and 2) trust – that it *will* work, that you *can* flip it, that sometimes what is upside down is really right side up. Serve with a big green salad for a complete meal.

Serves 4

250g giant/pearl
  couscous
320ml boiling water
10 spring onions, *trimmed and left whole (150g)*
120ml olive oil
150g baby spinach
1 tbsp coriander seeds, *toasted and roughly crushed with a pestle and mortar*
100g low-moisture
  mozzarella, *roughly grated*
50g pecorino, *finely grated, plus extra, finely grated, to serve*
2 garlic cloves, *crushed*
15g basil leaves, *roughly torn, plus a handful of picked leaves to serve*
220g Greek-style yoghurt
2 eggs
50g plain flour

PEPPER SAUCE
2 red peppers *(320g), seeds and stems discarded and each pepper quartered (280g)*
1 tomato, *halved (100g)*
60ml olive oil, *plus extra for drizzling*
2 large heads of garlic, *skin on and top ⅛ trimmed to expose the cloves*
1½ tbsp red wine vinegar
1 tsp maple syrup
salt and black pepper

1. Preheat the oven to 200°C fan. Put the peppers and tomato on a medium, parchment-lined baking tray and toss them together with 1 tablespoon of oil, ¼ teaspoon of salt and a good grind of pepper. Drizzle the garlic heads with a little oil, wrap tightly in foil and place them to one side of the tray. Roast for 35 minutes, or until the pepper skins are well charred and the garlic has softened.

2. Peel and discard the pepper and tomato skins and put the flesh into a food processor. Squeeze the garlic cloves out of their papery skins and add them to the machine along with the vinegar, maple syrup, ¼ teaspoon of salt and a good grind of pepper. Blitz for a few seconds, then, with the machine running, slowly drizzle in the remaining 3 tablespoons of oil until the sauce is homogenised and smooth.

3. Meanwhile, put the couscous, ½ teaspoon of salt and the boiling water into a medium saucepan on a medium-high heat. Bring to a simmer, cover with a lid and turn the heat to medium-low. Cook for 10 minutes, then remove the lid and set aside to cool.

4. Place a large non-stick frying pan on a high heat. Toss the spring onions in ½ tablespoon of oil and fry in the hot pan for 4 minutes, turning halfway, until softened and lightly charred. Set the spring onions aside. Turn the heat down to medium-high, then add another ½ tablespoon of oil and the spinach to the pan. Cook for 90 seconds to wilt, then transfer to a large bowl.

5. Roughly chop the spring onions and add two-thirds to the spinach bowl. Add the cooked couscous, crushed coriander seeds, both cheeses, the garlic, basil, yoghurt, eggs, flour, ½ teaspoon of salt and a good grind of pepper and mix together well.

6. Wipe out the frying pan and add 5 tablespoons of oil on a medium-high heat. Once hot, add the couscous mixture, using a spoon to evenly distribute. Turn the heat down to medium and cook for 18 minutes – the edges will start to turn golden and you should be able to loosen the cake from the base. Use a spatula to gently separate the cake from the sides of the pan, running it under the cake to try to loosen it from the bottom. Remove the pan from the heat and, very gently, invert the whole thing on to a large plate.

7. Add a tablespoon of oil to the pan and slide the cake back into it, crispy side up, to brown the other side. Cook for 8 minutes, on a medium heat, before sliding the cake on to a large wooden board or serving platter.

8. In a small bowl, combine the remaining chopped spring onions with the extra basil leaves and the last tablespoon of oil. Sprinkle the cake with the extra pecorino and top with the spring onion mixture. Serve the pepper sauce in a bowl alongside.

Make it your own:
- Leftover cooked rice or pearl barley, Parmesan and Gruyère, dill or tarragon, toasted cumin or fennel seeds, the options to MIYO are endless.
- Double up on the sauce – it makes a great vegan pasta sauce.

On black limes

More often than not, our cupboards will contain a few obscure ingredients: things you buy for that one recipe, pack away and then, well, forget about. Black limes are pretty obscure for some; you might have even bought a packet for an Ottolenghi recipe asking you to use them. We get it; they can be intimidating if you don't know what to do with them – bitter, astringent, mysterious, to say the least. What even are black limes? Well, they're limes that have been treated with a salt-water solution before being left out to dry in the sun, until completely dehydrated and very dark. Also called Omani limes, loomi aswad or noomi basra, they're a staple ingredient throughout the Persian Gulf, adding an earthy, bitter depth to the dishes they're used in. If you can't find dried black limes, then you can also use the lighter-coloured dried limes, which have more of a greeny-brown hue. Besides their different colouring, the two are pretty much interchangeable. You can use plenty of lime juice and zest as a substitute for dried limes, but in truth, their unique properties are unparalleled. If there's one funky ingredient we want you to pull out of the very back of your cupboards, or maybe even – dare we say – to add to your cupboards, it's a bag of black limes. They last for ever, and oh do they pack a punch.

A few black lime hacks:

• Throw them whole into soups and stews, adding a subtle astringent tang. Make sure to poke a few holes in them first – this will help them soften and release their flavour into the liquid they're cooked in.

• Blitz them into a powder to use in rubs and marinades. A coffee or spice grinder is best for this, ensuring the smoothest texture. To help this along, use the palm of your hand to lightly crush the black limes before blitzing.

• Decrease bitterness by removing the seeds, if you wish. Although this isn't really necessary.

• Use the black limes to make a sour tea called 'chai loomi'. Roughly break apart 3–4 limes and remove any seeds. Gently simmer in a litre of water for 10 minutes, then strain and add fresh mint, a squeeze of lemon juice, and sugar or honey to taste.

• Be sure to purchase black limes that are whole and not ground. You can grind them in a coffee or spice grinder as and when you need to, and they'll keep for much longer.

Black lime beef skewers with sumac onions

Prep time: *15 minutes*
Cook time: *25 minutes*
Marinating time: *1 hour to overnight*

Black limes act as both a flavour enhancer and a tenderiser in this marinade, softening the meat but also giving it an edgy tang. This dish is native to Bahrain and is locally called 'tikka', but is not really tikka as we know it to be. Grilled to order, the tikka comes wrapped up in a little flatbread bundle with raw onion, local rocket (called 'jarjeer') and lime wedges to squeeze on top. Be sure to source meat with some fat attached – this truly adds to the whole authentic eating experience. We urge you to give this marinade a go, if not with beef then with lamb, chicken, tofu or meaty mushrooms. Serve this with the roasted potatoes with aïoli (p. 78).

Serves 4

4 sirloin steaks *(1kg), with some fat attached*

5–6 dried black limes *(p. 50), roughly chopped, then finely ground in a coffee or spice grinder to get 3 tbsp*

2 lemons: *finely grate the zest to get 2 tsp and then juice to get 2½ tbsp*

1 tbsp ground cumin

6 garlic cloves, *crushed*

3 tbsp olive oil

sunflower oil, *for greasing*

4 naan or pita breads, *shop-bought or homemade (p. 23)*

1 tsp Aleppo chilli, *or ½ tsp regular chilli flakes*

5g picked parsley leaves

5g picked mint leaves

salt and black pepper

8 metal skewers, *about 25cm long, or wooden skewers soaked in water for 10 minutes*

SUMAC ONIONS

1 red onion, *thinly sliced (120g)*

1½ tsp sumac

¾ tbsp cider vinegar

1. Place the steaks between two pieces of baking parchment and use a mallet or the bottom of a saucepan to bash them until they're about 2cm thick. Cut the steaks, fat and all, into 2cm cubes and place them in a bowl with the ground black lime, lemon zest and juice, cumin, garlic, 2 tablespoons of olive oil, 1½ teaspoons of salt and a good grind of pepper. Leave to marinate for at least 1 hour, or refrigerate overnight.

2. For the sumac onions, mix the onion, sumac, vinegar and ⅛ teaspoon of salt together and leave to soften for at least 30 minutes.

3. Thread the beef on to the skewers, packing the cubes closely together.

4. Heat a well-greased griddle pan on a high heat. Once smoking and very hot, cook the skewers in batches for about 3–4 minutes per batch, until charred but not overcooked, turning as necessary. Transfer to a baking tray and cover with foil to keep warm.

5. Warm the bread in the hot griddle pan for about 30 seconds on each side.

6. Lay the bread out on a platter and top with the skewers, brushing them with the remaining tablespoon of olive oil and sprinkling with the chilli. Nestle the herbs to one side and serve with the sumac onions.

Make it your own:

- Use different fatty cuts of beef, lamb or chicken, or vegetables.
- Swap the black limes out for the lighter, Iranian dried limes.

Sesame-crusted feta with black lime honey syrup

Prep time: *15 minutes*
Cook time: *30 minutes*
Chilling time: *30 minutes to overnight*

'Everything is betta with feta,' says Tara, voted the number one feta fan of all time, and, to be fair, she might be right. We try really hard not to show cheese favouritism (cheesism), but we'd be lying if we didn't admit that feta makes a prominent appearance in the OTK fridge, its salty, tangy properties lending it well to multiple preparations.

This dish is a little bit sweet, a lotta bit salty, a tiny bit bitter and a whole bit crispy. It's exactly what you'd serve for brunch (with bacon, if you like) and not much else, as it really is quite rich.

Serves 8

2 blocks of Greek feta (360g), *each cut into 4 triangles (8 triangles in total)*
35g rice flour (or plain flour if gluten-free flour not needed)
1 large egg, *well beaten*
100g mixed black and white sesame seeds, *lightly toasted*
2 tbsp olive oil
½ tbsp picked lemon thyme leaves, *or regular thyme leaves*

SYRUP
120g runny honey
1 tsp ground black lime (p. 50) (optional)
3 lemons: *1 juiced to get 1 tbsp and the other 2 left whole*

Get ahead:
– Coat the feta the night before, cover well and keep refrigerated.

1. Line a shallow baking dish (or baking tray with a slight lip), about 30cm x 20cm in size, with baking parchment.

2. Pat dry the feta pieces, then dip each piece in the flour, gently shaking off the excess. Coat in the egg, followed by the sesame seeds, making sure the feta pieces are completely coated. Transfer each piece to your prepared dish and refrigerate for at least 30 minutes, or longer if time allows.

3. Preheat the oven to 220°C fan. Drizzle the coated feta pieces with the oil and bake from cold, for 18 minutes, very gently flipping the pieces over halfway, or until golden and warmed through.

4. While the feta is baking, put the honey and black lime, if using, into a small saucepan on a medium-high heat. Once it starts to bubble, turn the heat to medium and cook, stirring occasionally, until it turns a deep amber caramel, about 6–7 minutes. Take off the heat and stir in the lemon juice. Set aside to cool for 5 minutes.

5. Use a small, sharp knife to peel and segment the remaining two lemons and stir the segments into the cooled honey mixture.

6. When ready, pour the lemon syrup directly over the feta in the baking dish, sprinkle with the thyme and serve at once, straight from the dish.

Make it your own:
– Leave out the black lime if you can't find any – this dish is just as special without it.
– Swap out the feta for halloumi cheese instead.

Tabbouleh fritters with quick chilli sauce

Prep time: *25 minutes*
Cook time: *45 minutes*

You can choose to eat these as they are or, for the ultimate veggie pita, make the homemade pitas on p. 23, open them up into a pocket, and stuff them with these fritters, the chilli sauce, tahini sauce (p. 27) and some raw veggies. Make sure you have some napkins handy!

Makes 8 fritters to serve 4

70g bulgur wheat

200g baby spinach

50g parsley, *roughly chopped*

20g picked mint leaves

½ red onion, *roughly chopped (60g)*

1 garlic clove, *roughly chopped*

1 tsp ground allspice

1 tsp ground cinnamon

1 tbsp finely grated lemon zest

75ml olive oil

3 large eggs

salt and black pepper

QUICK CHILLI SAUCE

3 tbsp olive oil

2 garlic cloves, *roughly chopped*

½ onion, *roughly chopped (75g)*

4 tsp tomato paste

2 red chillies, *roughly chopped, seeds and all (20g)*

2 vine tomatoes, *roughly chopped, seeds and all (200g)*

1½ tbsp apple cider vinegar

1. Put the bulgur wheat into a small saucepan with 75ml of water and ¼ teaspoon of salt. Bring to the boil, cover with a lid, then remove from the heat. Leave to sit and steam gently, covered, for 10 minutes, then fluff up with a fork. Allow to cool.

2. Meanwhile, make the chilli sauce by heating the oil in a small frying pan on a medium-high heat. Add the garlic and onion and cook for 5 minutes, stirring occasionally, until softened and lightly coloured. Add the tomato paste and cook for 1 minute more, stirring continuously, then add the chillies and remove from the heat. Leave to cool for 5 minutes, then transfer to a food processor and pulse a few times until finely chopped. Add the tomatoes, vinegar and the ½ teaspoon of salt and pulse to a semi-smooth purée.

3. Blanch the spinach in plenty of boiling water for just 20 seconds. Drain, running under cold water, then squeeze out as much liquid as possible. You need 90g.

4. Put the cooled bulgur wheat, blanched spinach, herbs, red onion, garlic, spices, lemon zest, 1 tablespoon of oil, ¾ teaspoon of salt and a good grind of pepper into the food processor and pulse a couple of times, until finely chopped. Add the eggs and pulse a few times more, until just combined. Transfer the batter to a jug or bowl.

5. Heat the remaining 4 tablespoons of oil in a large sauté pan on a medium-high heat. Add large spoonfuls of the batter to the pan and gently shape to form 6–7cm patties about 2cm thick. Fry 3–4 at a time, about 2–3 minutes per side, to make eight in total. Turn down the heat if they get too dark.

6. Serve the fritters warm, with the quick chilli sauce alongside.

Spiced semolina with sweetcorn, peanuts and coriander

Prep time: *15 minutes*
Cook time: *20 minutes*

Semolina is, more often than not, overlooked in favour of its similar-natured cousin polenta. They can both be used for the same purposes really, making wonderful desserts and breads or eaten warm as a side. That being said, they are distant cousins (twice removed), and therefore still have their own individual attributes – with semolina being slightly creamier, especially when cooked in this porridge-like way. Make sure to source the medium to coarse semolina and not the super-fine one. Serve as a brunch, or for dinner with some grilled prawns or tofu.

Serves 4

3 tbsp olive oil

½ tsp black mustard seeds

1 tsp cumin seeds

½ tsp ground cinnamon

2 whole cloves

350g sweetcorn kernels (from 2–3 cobs), or the frozen equivalent, defrosted

1 green chilli, *finely chopped, seeds and all (10g)*

¼ tsp asafoetida

60g roasted and salted peanuts

2–3 limes: *1–2 juiced to get 2 tbsp, and the other cut into 4 wedges to serve*

20g fresh ginger, *peeled and finely grated*

2 garlic cloves, *crushed*

200ml full-fat coconut milk, *plus 2 tbsp extra to serve*

¼ tsp ground turmeric

75g medium to coarse semolina

5g picked fresh coriander leaves, *with some stem attached*

salt

1. Put a tablespoon of oil into a large sauté pan on a medium-high heat. Add the mustard seeds, cumin seeds, cinnamon and cloves and fry for about 30–60 seconds, until the seeds start to pop. Add the sweetcorn, half the chilli, the asafoetida and ½ teaspoon of salt and cook for 3 minutes, stirring occasionally, until fragrant. Add the peanuts and cook for 3 minutes more, or until the mixture takes on some colour. Off the heat, add the lime juice and discard the cloves.

2. Transfer half the sweetcorn mixture to a food processor and blitz to a coarse paste. Set both sweetcorn mixtures aside, separately, until ready to use.

3. Put the remaining 2 tablespoons of oil into a medium saucepan and put on a medium-high heat. Add the ginger, garlic and remaining green chilli and fry for 90 seconds, until fragrant. Add 400ml of water, the coconut milk, turmeric and ¾ teaspoon of salt and bring to the boil.

4. Once boiling, reduce the heat to medium and slowly add the semolina, whisking constantly to avoid any lumps.

Continue to whisk for 3 minutes, until the consistency is that of thin porridge. Add the blitzed sweetcorn mixture and cook for 1 minute, stirring constantly, until thickened slightly.

5. Divide the porridge between four bowls and drizzle with the extra coconut milk. Mix the coriander leaves into the sautéd sweetcorn mix and spoon this over the top. Serve warm with a lime wedge.

Make it your own:

- Asafoetida is a pungent onion-garlicky spice used a lot in southern Indian cooking. Leave it out if you can't find any; it's still just as good without.
- Play with your nuts and spices!
- Use quick-cook polenta instead of semolina, adjusting liquid levels accordingly.

_____

_____

_____

Veg

Your

BOX

Your veg box

There's no secret that the OTK crew stand faithfully behind Yotam's love affair with vegetables. We have an all-inclusive, every-vegetable-counts policy, which sometimes means that narrowing the options down can prove difficult. We therefore stuck to the most accessible vegetables as we ate and tested our way through the seasons, while keeping the 'make it your own' options as expansive as possible. Big bundles of herbs and plenty of leafy greens, a few aubergines, a bag of onions and a very large butternut squash. If these were the contents of your veg box, what would you do with it all?

Focusing on the culinary positives of recent times, many of us have upped the hours we spend in the kitchen cooking for ourselves and our households. We've also spent some time digging through veg box deliveries, or rummaging through the season's finds at our local (but also not always fully stocked) greengrocer or supermarket. This has sometimes meant less choice to play with on the one hand, but also way more perishable goods to reckon with on the other.

In this chapter, we aim to help you navigate through your vegetable finds while also keeping a few things in mind. The first is frugality – the need to use up what's on hand: a few flimsy-looking aubergines soon become burnt aubergine, tomato and tahini (p. 83). The second is creativity, or more likely an aversion to monotony, turning sweet potato flesh into shakshuka and saving the skins for a crispy snack (p. 84). The last is mindfulness, of perfectly imperfect produce, the 'whats' of what's in season and the 'hows' of how best to use them – using funky-looking tomatoes in the not-your-average tomato salad (p. 67). All the while we invite you to substitute and swap out, finding innovative solutions to leave your own mark on these dishes.

This is a journey through our veg boxes, embracing the multitude of ways in which we treat our vegetables – smooshed, grated, grilled, roasted – and the various ways in which we serve them – with eggs, on warm yoghurt, spooned on to bread, etc. – helping you answer the question 'What will I do with my veg box?'

Green herb bagna cauda

Prep time: *35 minutes*
Cook time: *45 minutes*

This dip is loosely based on bagna càuda, an Italian dish made from anchovies, garlic and olive oil. Here we add earthy cooked herbs and vibrant fresh ones – increasing the dip's savoury intensity and making it perfect for crudités. We like using up all the bits in our seasonal veg box as little vehicles to scoop and eat with, but you could just as easily serve this with crackers or crusty bread.

Serves 6, as a snack

200ml olive oil, *plus extra for drizzling*

2 onions, *halved and thinly sliced (300g)*

70g parsley, *roughly chopped*

70g fresh coriander, *roughly chopped*

50g dill, *roughly chopped*

6 spring onions, *finely sliced (75g)*

½ tsp ground turmeric

2 tsp cumin seeds, *roughly crushed with a pestle and mortar*

15 garlic cloves, *peeled*

12 anchovies packed in olive oil, *drained (40g)*

75ml lemon juice

20g picked mint leaves

salt and black pepper

ANY-STYLE CRUDITÉS

1 Italian radicchio trevisano *(or red endive), leaves separated*

150g baby carrots, *peeled and halved lengthways*

100g sugar snap peas, *stringy bits removed*

150g rainbow or breakfast radishes, *halved*

1. Put 3 tablespoons of oil into a large sauté pan on a medium-high heat. Once hot, cook the onions for 12–15 minutes, stirring, until softened and browned. Transfer half the onions and oil to a bowl and return the pan to a medium heat. Add 50g each of the parsley and coriander, 40g of the dill and all the spring onions, and cook, stirring often, for 15 minutes, or until deeply green and fragrant, but not browned. Add the spices and cook for 3 minutes more. Set aside to cool.

2. Meanwhile, put the garlic and the remaining 155ml of oil into a small saucepan, for which you have a lid. Place on a medium-low heat, covered, and cook for 10 minutes, stirring once, until the garlic has started to soften. Add the anchovies, replace the lid and cook for 10 minutes more. Remove from the heat and leave to cool.

3. Put the herb mixture and garlic mixture into a food processor along with the lemon juice, mint, the remaining parsley, coriander and dill, ¼ teaspoon of salt and a good grind of pepper, and blitz until smooth.

4. Transfer to a bowl and top with the reserved browned onions, stirring them through a little. Place on a board and arrange the crudités all around. Lastly, drizzle the crudités with a little oil and season them lightly with salt and pepper.

Make it your own:
– Use up whatever mixture of soft herbs and spring onions you have, so long as it comes to 265g worth of herbage.
– Veganise it: swap out the anchovies for 2 tablespoons of capers.

Not-your-average tomato salad

Prep time: *20 minutes*
Cook time: *40 minutes*

The flavourful dressing is what makes this salad so unique, thanks to the infused ginger and garlic oil which certifiably takes your tomato salad game to beyond average. Use whatever mixture of tomatoes you can find, making sure they're wonderfully ripe and in season. Make this salad vegan by swapping out the fish sauce for light soy sauce, adjusting salt levels accordingly.

Serves 4, as a side

5 garlic cloves, *thinly sliced*

35g fresh ginger, *peeled and julienned*

135ml olive oil

3–4 limes: *finely grate the zest to get 1 tbsp and then juice to get 3 tbsp*

2 tbsp fish sauce

10g fresh coriander leaves, *roughly chopped*

500g heirloom tomatoes, *cored and cut into 1½cm-thick slices*

300g mixed cherry tomatoes *(red/yellow/ orange), halved lengthways*

½ red onion, *cut into thin rounds (60g)*

flaked sea salt and black pepper

1. Put the garlic, ginger, oil and ½ teaspoon of flaked sea salt into a small sauté pan and place it on a medium-low heat. Cook gently for 25 minutes, swirling the pan occasionally, until the solids are lightly golden. Strain the oil through a sieve set over a bowl and set aside to cool for 10 minutes. Transfer the solids to a plate lined with kitchen paper to crisp up further.

2. Use a fork to whisk the lime zest, lime juice, fish sauce and coriander into the cooled ginger-garlic oil until combined.

3. Gently toss all the tomatoes together with 1 teaspoon of flaked sea salt and a generous grind of pepper. Arrange the tomatoes and red onion on a large platter and spoon over the dressing, followed by the crispy ginger and garlic. Serve right away.

Smooshed carrots with coriander-pistachio pesto and pickled onions

Prep time: *25 minutes*
Cook time: *1 hour 15 minutes*

Think big, bold colours and flavours: this dish is a good way to dress up the humble carrot in its most fantastic party attire. Serve this as part of a mezze spread or as a side to your protein of choice.

Serves 4, as a side or part of a mezze spread

½ **small red onion,** *finely chopped (50g)*

2 **tbsp lime juice**

1.2kg **carrots,** *peeled and cut widthways into 3–4cm chunks*

135ml **olive oil**

¾ **tsp ground turmeric**

7 **garlic cloves,** *peeled, 6 left whole and 1 crushed*

2 **tsp coriander seeds,** *roughly crushed with a pestle and mortar*

2 **tsp cumin seeds,** *roughly crushed with a pestle and mortar*

½ **tsp chilli flakes**

1½ **tbsp maple or agave syrup**

20g **fresh coriander,** *roughly chopped*

2 **spring onions,** *thinly sliced (30g)*

40g **pistachios,** *very lightly toasted and roughly chopped*

60g **Greek-style yoghurt**

salt and black pepper

1. Preheat the oven to 180°C fan.

2. In a small bowl, mix together the onion, 1 tablespoon of lime juice and a pinch of salt and set aside to pickle.

3. Put the carrots, 4 tablespoons of oil, the turmeric, 200ml of water, ½ teaspoon of salt and a good grind of pepper into a medium roasting tin or baking dish and mix everything together. Roast for 25 minutes, then add the whole garlic cloves and the spices and return to the oven for another 20 minutes, or until the carrots are cooked through. Turn the oven temperature up to 210°C fan, drizzle the carrots all over with the maple or agave syrup, and return to the oven for 10 minutes, or until the carrots have taken on a little colour. Leave to cool for about 5 minutes, then use a fork or potato masher to smoosh the carrots into a coarse mash (you don't want it super smooth).

4. Meanwhile, make the pesto. Put the fresh coriander, spring onions, pistachios, 3 tablespoons of oil, crushed garlic, ¼ teaspoon of salt and a good grind of pepper into a food processor and blitz to a coarse paste. Transfer the pesto to a medium bowl and stir in the last 2 tablespoons of oil.

5. Make the lime yoghurt by combining the yoghurt with the remaining tablespoon of lime juice in a small bowl.

6. Spread the carrot mash out on a large plate and dot with spoonfuls of the yoghurt, followed by about two-thirds of the pesto (serving the remainder alongside). Finally, top with the pickled onion and serve warm or at room temperature.

Make it your own:
- No carrots? No problem. Use sweet potatoes or butternut squash instead.
- Swap out coriander for parsley, and pistachios for pine nuts or almonds.
- Veganise it: leave out the lime yoghurt, or use a non-dairy yoghurt instead.

(All the) herb dumplings with caramelised onions

Prep time: *25 minutes*
Cook time: *1 hour 30 minutes*

We love the abundance of herbs at play here, which lends a deep earthiness to these dumplings. Cooking down the herbs in this way is a technique quite distinct to the Middle East, where herbs are used liberally as a base for soups and stews, adding bulk and heft, rather than as a finishing touch. When cooking herbs, patience is key: cook them on a moderate heat and stir often; they'll start to lose their vibrancy and become wonderfully fragrant and deeply green, adding a whole other dimension to your dishes. They're only cooked here for 20 minutes or so, but could go for much longer, intensifying with time. Feel free to play around with the herbs if you wish, using more or less of your choosing, depending on what you have. The real star of the dish, though, is the onions, cooked low and slow with saffron and cardamom and a generous amount of butter. Serve this alongside a summery salad and some crusty bread, for a complete meal.

Serves 4, as a starter or side

1kg onions *(about 5–6),*
halved and sliced ½cm thick

10 cardamom pods, *roughly*
bashed open with a pestle
and mortar

60ml olive oil

110g unsalted butter, *at*
room temperature

4 garlic cloves, *crushed*

100g fresh coriander,
roughly chopped

100g parsley, *roughly*
chopped

70g dill, *roughly chopped*

30g tarragon leaves, *roughly*
chopped

7 spring onions, *thinly*
sliced (105g)

1½ tsp cumin seeds, *roughly*
crushed with a pestle and
mortar

¾ tsp ground turmeric

50g whole-mIlk ricotta

100g Greek feta, *roughly*
crumbled

60g Parmesan, *finely grated*

1 large egg

70g plain flour

⅓ tsp saffron threads,
roughly crushed

2 tbsp lemon juice

salt and black pepper

1. Preheat the oven to 180°C fan.

2. Put the onions, cardamom, half the oil, 40g of butter and 1 teaspoon of salt into a medium baking dish and mix together to combine. Bake for 60–70 minutes, stirring 4–5 times during, until softened and nicely caramelised.

3. Meanwhile, heat the remaining 2 tablespoons of oil in a large, non-stick sauté pan on a medium heat. Add the herbs and spring onions and cook, stirring often, for about 10 minutes. Add the cumin and turmeric and cook for 10 minutes more, or until the herbs are deeply green and fragrant. Set aside to cool.

4. Beat together the ricotta, feta, 50g of the Parmesan, the egg, 1 teaspoon of salt and plenty of pepper in a large bowl. Add the flour and the cooled herb mixture and mix well. Refrigerate to set, about 20–40 minutes. Use your hands to roll into 12 compact dumplings, about 45–50g each.

5. Bring a large pot of water to the boil, then turn the heat down to a bare simmer on a medium heat. Drop in the dumplings and cook for 10–12 minutes, or until they rise to the surface and have cooked through the centre. Use a slotted spoon to gently transfer the dumplings to a tray lined with kitchen paper, to dry.

6. When the onions are ready and hot from the oven, add the remaining 70g of butter, the saffron and the lemon juice and mix everything to combine. Turn the oven temperature up to 200°C fan.

7. Top the onions with the dumplings, slightly spaced apart, then sprinkle all over with the remaining 10g of Parmesan. Return to the oven for 8–10 minutes, or until everything is bubbling and warmed through.

Make it your own:

– Use any mixture of herbs you have on hand, using more or less of what you like.

– You can swap out the herbs for spinach, cooking it just enough to release any water. Make sure you then wring it well.

_____

_____

Spiced mashed aubergine and peas

Prep time: *25 minutes*
Cook time: *40 minutes*

More often than not, staff food at the Ottolenghi delis uses up leftover roasted vegetables, mixed with some of our abundance of spices to make different types of curries. Roasted aubergines are therefore in regular rotation on the staff food menu, the mighty aubergine a core part of what makes Ottolenghi, well . . . Ottolenghi. This is a very loose take on baingan bharta, an Indian mashed aubergine dish. On quieter days, a few treasured staff have whipped up some homemade roti to serve alongside, but more often than not we'll have this with plain rice.

Serves 4

3 aubergines *(750g), stems discarded and flesh roughly cut into 3–4cm cubes*
120ml olive oil
150g cherry tomatoes
1 red onion, *thinly sliced (120g)*
6 garlic cloves, *crushed*
30g fresh ginger, *peeled and finely chopped*
1 green chilli, *finely chopped, seeds and all*
1 tsp black mustard seeds
1 tsp ground turmeric
1 tsp garam masala
1 tsp ground cumin
150g tinned plum tomatoes *(about ⅔ of a tin), roughly crushed by hand*
20g fresh coriander, *roughly chopped*
2 tbsp lemon juice
200g frozen peas, *defrosted*
3 spring onions, *finely sliced at an angle (30g)*
2 tbsp Greek-style yoghurt
salt and black pepper

1. Preheat the oven to 220°C fan. Toss the aubergine pieces together with 4 tablespoons of oil, ¾ teaspoon of salt and a good grind of pepper on a large, parchment-lined baking tray, and roast for 20 minutes. Add the cherry tomatoes, giving everything a stir, and return to the oven for another 10 minutes, until the tomatoes have blistered and the aubergine is deeply golden.

2. Meanwhile, make the sauce. Put 2 tablespoons of oil into a large sauté pan on a medium-high heat. Add the onion and cook for 7 minutes, stirring occasionally, until nicely browned. Add the garlic, ginger and chilli and cook for 2 minutes more, until fragrant, then add the spices and cook for 30 seconds. Add the tinned tomatoes, 300ml of water, ½ teaspoon of salt and plenty of pepper, and bring to a simmer.

Lower the heat to medium and cook for 15 minutes, stirring every now and then, until thick and rich. Stir in two-thirds of the coriander, 1 tablespoon of lemon juice and the roasted vegetables and use a fork to roughly mash every together.

3. In a separate bowl, toss together the peas, the remaining coriander, the spring onions, 1 tablespoon of oil, ¼ teaspoon of salt and a good grind of pepper.

4. In a small bowl, combine the yoghurt with a pinch of salt and the remaining tablespoon of lemon juice.

5. Transfer the mashed aubergine to a serving plate and top with the pea mixture. Drizzle all over with the yoghurt and the remaining tablespoon of oil, and serve warm.

Make it your own:

- Veganise it: drizzle with a little coconut milk in place of the yoghurt.
- Play with your spices. It's okay if you don't have them all! Use more or less of what you do have.

_____

_____

Grilled courgettes with warm yoghurt and saffron butter

Prep time: *10 minutes*
Cook time: *30 minutes*

This recipe is inspired by kousa b'laban, a Levantine dish of stuffed baby marrow cooked in yoghurt. In this simplified version the yoghurt sauce and grilled courgettes are cooked separately, then served with a quick saffron butter to spoon on top.

There's a bit of an art to cooking yoghurt without having it curdle; stabilisers such as cornflour and egg yolk tend to do the trick, as does cooking the yoghurt on a moderate heat, stirring continuously and gently warming through without boiling. The result: a silky-smooth and tangy sauce, great for these courgettes but also with other grilled veggies, fatty meats or even as a sauce to pasta.

Serves 2–4

30g unsalted butter

¼ tsp saffron threads, *roughly crushed*

4 small, pale green or regular courgettes, *tops trimmed slightly and courgettes halved lengthways (600g)*

2½ tbsp olive oil

1 tsp cornflour

300g Greek-style yoghurt

2 garlic cloves, *crushed*

½ tsp dried mint

¾ tsp coriander seeds, *toasted and roughly crushed with a pestle and mortar*

1½ tbsp picked mint leaves

½ lemon

salt and black pepper

1. Preheat the oven to a high grill setting.

2. Put the butter and saffron into a small saucepan on a medium heat. When the butter has melted, set aside to infuse.

3. Place the courgettes on a parchment-lined baking tray and toss with 2 tablespoons of oil, ⅓ teaspoon of salt and a good grind of pepper. Arrange them cut side up and grill for 15–20 minutes, until nicely charred and softened.

4. Towards the last 10 minutes of grilling time, make the sauce. In a large bowl, whisk together the cornflour and 3 tablespoons of water until smooth, then add the yoghurt, garlic, dried mint, the remaining ½ tablespoon of oil and ½ teaspoon of salt. Whisk to combine, then transfer to a large, non-stick sauté pan on a medium heat. Cook, stirring continuously, for about 10 minutes, or until thickened slightly and warmed through. Do not let the sauce boil, or it will split.

5. Transfer the warm yoghurt sauce to a plate with a lip and top with the courgettes, grilled side up. Spoon over the saffron butter, then sprinkle with the coriander seeds and mint leaves. Squeeze over the lemon half and serve right away.

Make it your own:
– No saffron? Use a pinch of turmeric instead.

_____

_____

Roasted pepper salad with cucumber and herbs

Prep time: *20 minutes*
Cook time: *40 minutes*

This is a take on Tunisian mechouia, a grilled vegetable salad to which we've added fresh cucumber and herbs. You can eat this warm or at room temperature, as a starter or side. It also works well spooned into a sandwich, with plenty of peppery rocket and a good glug of olive oil. A special shout-out to Paula Wolfert and her beautifully informative book *The Food of Morocco*, which makes a sneaky appearance in this photo.

Serves 4, as a starter or side

4 green peppers *(600g), stems and seeds discarded, and flesh cut into roughly 4cm pieces*

2 red peppers *(300g), stems and seeds discarded, and flesh cut into roughly 4cm pieces*

4 vine tomatoes *(400g), each cut into quarters*

2 small red onions *(200g), cut into roughly 3cm pieces*

1 green chilli, *stem removed and left whole (10g)*

6 large garlic cloves, *peeled*

90ml olive oil

1½ tbsp lemon juice

10g parsley, *roughly chopped*

10g fresh coriander, *roughly chopped*

1 cucumber, *peeled, deseeded and cut into 1cm cubes (330g)*

¾ tsp Urfa chilli, *or regular chilli flakes*

salt and black pepper

1. Preheat the oven to 230°C fan.

2. In a large bowl, toss together both peppers, the tomatoes, onions, chilli, garlic, 4 tablespoons of oil, ¾ teaspoon of salt and a good grind of pepper. Spread out on two large, parchment-lined baking trays and roast for about 30 minutes, stirring once or twice during cooking, until the vegetables are softened and charred.

3. Once cool enough to handle, coarsely chop the vegetables into a chunky mash and transfer to a bowl along with the lemon juice, herbs, ½ teaspoon of salt and a good grind of pepper.

4. In a separate, medium bowl, toss the cucumber with the remaining 2 tablespoons of oil, ¼ teaspoon of salt and a grind of pepper.

5. Spread the roasted pepper mixture on a plate. Spoon over the cucumber and sprinkle with the chilli.

Make it your own:
- Keep this kid-friendly by eliminating or reducing the amount of chilli.
- Swap out the cucumber for another crunchy veg, such as celery or kohlrabi.

_____

_____

_____

Roasted potatoes with aïoli and buttered pine nuts

Prep time: *10 minutes*
Cook time: *50 minutes*

Kebab shop 'chips with mayo' are the inspiration for this dish, although this version is a little more involved. There's a generous sauce-to-potato ratio here, which is kind of naughty, but also what you really, truly want. This goes really well with the black lime beef skewers (p. 52).

Serves 4, as a side

750g baby new potatoes, *skin on and halved lengthways*

2 tbsp olive oil

5g parsley, *roughly chopped*

salt and black pepper

AÏOLI

2 large garlic cloves, *crushed*

1 tsp Dijon mustard

1 large egg, *plus 1 yolk*

100ml olive oil

100ml sunflower oil

1 tbsp lemon juice

75g Greek-style yoghurt

BUTTERED PINE NUTS

30g unsalted butter

20g pine nuts

¼ tsp smoked paprika

1. Preheat the oven to 220°C fan.

2. Put the potatoes and 2 teaspoons of salt into a medium saucepan and pour over plenty of cold water, to cover by about 4cm. Place on a medium-high heat, bring to the boil, then simmer for 6 minutes, or until the potatoes are almost cooked through but still with a bite. Drain them in a sieve and pat dry, then transfer to a parchment-lined baking tray and toss with the oil, ⅓ teaspoon of salt and a good grind of pepper. Roast, stirring once or twice, for 35 minutes, or until deeply golden. Stir through the parsley.

3. Meanwhile, make the aïoli by putting the garlic, mustard, egg, yolk and ¼ teaspoon of salt into the small bowl of a food processor and blitzing until combined, about 10 seconds. With the machine still running, add both oils in a very slow and steady stream, until you have a loose, mayonnaise-like consistency. Transfer to a bowl, stir in the lemon juice and yoghurt and set aside (or refrigerate) until needed.

4. Put the butter into a small sauté pan on a medium heat. Once melted, add the pine nuts and cook until golden, about 3–4 minutes. Stir through the paprika, then remove from the heat and transfer to a bowl.

5. Spread the aïoli out on a round shallow platter. Top with the warm potatoes and spoon over the buttered pine nuts.

Make it your own:
- If you can't get hold of baby new potatoes, just use regular new potatoes and cut them into 1½cm slices.
- Play with your nuts. Roughly chopped blanched almonds or hazelnuts would be great here!
- Veganise it: use chickpea mayo (p. 32) instead, and olive oil in place of the butter.

_____

_____

_____

Summer courgettes with tomatoes and ricotta

Prep time: *25 minutes*
Cook time: *25 minutes*

There are no tricks here, no clever Ottolenghi twists or obscure ingredients. This is a fairly simple dish that tastes like an Italian summer holiday, and is a nod to the old adage that less is sometimes more. Use the best in-season produce you can find and eat it as is – it really is that good.

Serves 4, as a starter or side

3½ tbsp olive oil

5 garlic cloves, *finely sliced on a mandolin or by hand*

750g mixed green and yellow courgettes, *quartered lengthways, then cut into 2cm pieces*

5g oregano sprigs

3 strips finely shaved lemon skin

10g picked basil leaves

120g whole-milk ricotta

TOMATO SALSA

4 very ripe plum tomatoes, *finely chopped (400g)*

2 tsp finely chopped oregano leaves

1 tsp lemon juice

2 tbsp olive oil

1 small garlic clove, *crushed*

salt and black pepper

1. Mix all the ingredients for the tomato salsa together with ¼ teaspoon of salt and a good grind of pepper. Set aside.

2. Place a large, non-stick sauté pan on a medium-high heat with 2 tablespoons of oil and the garlic. Gently fry for 3 minutes, stirring often, until the garlic is soft and aromatic. You don't want it to brown at all, so turn the heat down if necessary.

3. Add the courgettes, oregano, lemon skin, 5g of basil leaves and ¾ teaspoon of salt. Cook for 15 minutes, stirring every now and then, until the courgettes are very soft, but still mostly holding their shape. You don't want the courgettes to brown, so turn the heat down if they do.

4. Remove the cooked basil, oregano and lemon skin from the courgettes and discard. Transfer the courgettes to a large plate with a lip. Spoon the tomato salsa evenly over the courgettes, then top with spoonfuls of the ricotta. Drizzle with the remaining 1½ tablespoons of oil and season with a pinch of salt. Finish with the remaining 5g of basil leaves and serve.

Make it your own:
- Swap out the ricotta for torn buffalo mozzarella.
- Veganise it: this tastes just as delicious without the cheese!

Burnt aubergine, tomato and tahini

Prep time: *20 minutes*
Cook time: *1 hour 10 minutes*

This dish was born out of some leftover tomato pasta sauce, as well as a few aubergines that really needed using up. Scoop this up with warm pita bread (p. 23) and eat it alongside other mezze, or with soft-boiled eggs for a hearty breakfast.

Serves 4, as part of a mezze spread

4 medium aubergines (1kg)

3 tbsp olive oil, *plus extra for greasing*

2 garlic cloves, *thinly sliced*

15g pine nuts

1½ tsp cumin seeds, *roughly crushed with a pestle and mortar*

1½ tsp coriander seeds, *roughly crushed with a pestle and mortar*

½ tsp chilli flakes

30g tahini

5g dill, *roughly chopped, plus 1 tbsp extra picked leaves to serve*

TOMATO SAUCE

3 tbsp olive oil

1 onion, *finely chopped (180g)*

4 garlic cloves, *crushed*

1 tsp tomato paste

1 tin of plum tomatoes (400g), *roughly crushed by hand*

½ tsp caster sugar

salt and black pepper

1. Place a well-greased griddle pan on a high heat. Prick the aubergines all over with a fork, about 8–10 times, and, once smoking, grill them, turning as necessary until well charred all over and softened through the middle, about 45 minutes. Set aside to cool completely and, once cool enough to handle, peel and discard the stems and skins (don't worry if there's some skin attached) and roughly pull apart the flesh into strands. Set aside.

2. Meanwhile, make the tomato sauce. Put the oil into a medium sauté pan on a medium-high heat. Add the onion and cook for 6 minutes, stirring occasionally, until softened and lightly coloured. Add the crushed garlic and tomato paste and cook for a minute more, then add the tinned tomatoes, sugar, 100ml of water, ½ teaspoon of salt and a generous grind of pepper. Bring to a simmer, then lower the heat to medium and cook for 18 minutes, stirring occasionally, until thick and rich.

3. Make the topping. Heat the oil in a small frying pan on a medium-high heat, then add the sliced garlic and the pine nuts and cook for 60–90 seconds, or until lightly golden. Add the spices and a tiny pinch of salt and immediately remove from the heat. Set aside.

4. In a small bowl, whisk the tahini with 2½ tablespoons of water and a tiny pinch of salt until smooth and pourable.

5. To the tomato sauce, add the burnt aubergine, 3 tablespoons of water, ¼ teaspoon of salt and a good grind of pepper and cook on a medium-high heat for about 5 minutes, stirring occasionally, until heated through. Remove from the heat and stir through the chopped dill. Drizzle all over with the tahini, then spoon over the fried garlic and pine nut mixture and top with the picked dill leaves. Serve warm.

> *Make it your own:*
> – Save time by using jarred tomato sauce instead.
> – Replace the burnt aubergine with chopped-up roasted veggies such as courgettes and red peppers.
>
> _____
>
> _____
>
> _____

Sweet potato shakshuka with sriracha butter and pickled onions

Prep time: *20 minutes*
Cook time: *1 hour 20 minutes*

A far cry from a classic shakshuka, yes, but we've found that sweet potatoes provide just the right amount of moisture and heft to serve as a base for these eggs. Serve this vibrant dish as a weekend brunch; it sure looks the part.

Serves 4

1kg sweet potatoes, *skin on and scrubbed clean*

1 small red onion, *thinly sliced into rounds (100g)*

2 tbsp lemon juice

3 tbsp olive oil

150g mature cheddar, *roughly grated*

3 garlic cloves, *crushed*

1 tsp cumin seeds, *roughly crushed with a pestle and mortar*

8 medium eggs

25g unsalted butter

¾ tbsp sriracha

2 tbsp picked fresh coriander leaves, *with some stem attached*

salt and black pepper

1. Preheat the oven to 200°C fan. Poke the sweet potatoes all over with a fork (about 8–10 times) and place them on a medium, parchment-lined baking tray. Bake for 45–50 minutes, or until cooked through and softened. Set aside to cool and turn the oven temperature down to 180°C fan.

2. Meanwhile, in a small bowl mix together the onion, 1 tablespoon of lemon juice and a pinch of salt and set aside to pickle.

3. Remove the cooked potato skins and tear them into roughly 4cm pieces. Transfer the potato flesh to a large bowl and set aside. Place the skins back on the baking tray and toss with 1 tablespoon of oil, ¼ teaspoon of salt and a good grind of pepper. Bake for 8 minutes, or until nicely coloured and starting to crisp up. Set aside to cool and crisp up further.

4. Use a fork to mash the potato flesh until smooth, then add the cheddar, garlic, cumin, another tablespoon of oil, the remaining tablespoon of lemon juice, 1 teaspoon of salt and a generous grind of pepper, and mix to combine.

5. Put the remaining tablespoon of oil into a large frying pan, for which you have a lid, and swirl around to coat the bottom. Spoon the mashed potato mixture into the pan, using your spoon to distribute it evenly. Place on a medium-high heat and leave to cook for about 7 minutes, for the bottom to start to colour. Turn the heat down to medium and use a spoon to make eight wells in the potato mixture, breaking an egg into each. Sprinkle lightly with salt and pepper, cover with the lid and cook for 4–5 minutes, rotating the pan, or until the whites are set and the yolks are still runny.

6. While the eggs are cooking, put the butter and sriracha into a small saucepan on a medium heat and cook until the butter has melted, whisking constantly to emulsify. Remove the mixture from the heat before it starts to bubble – you don't want it to split.

7. When ready, spoon the sriracha butter all over the eggs, then top with a good handful of the crispy potato skins, half the pickled onion and all the picked coriander leaves. Serve right away, with the rest of the potato skins and pickled onion to eat alongside.

Make it your own:
- Save time by cooking the sweet taters in the microwave instead.
- Use any kind of oozy melty cheese and any spice you like for the base.
- Experiment with other hot sauces, such as Tabasco or harissa.

_____

_____

_____

Grilled bread with tomato and fried garlic

Prep time: *10 minutes*
Cook time: *20 minutes*

This is a take on the wonderfully simple (but ever satisfying) Spanish pan con tomate. Beautifully ripe tomatoes and some stale bread are all you need to make this quick and easy starter or side.

Serves 4

6 garlic cloves, *5 thinly sliced and 1 crushed*

75ml olive oil, *plus extra for greasing and brushing*

850g ripe plum tomatoes

½ tsp chilli flakes

1 tbsp red wine vinegar

8 x 2cm-thick slices of stale ciabatta bread *(200g)*

150g datterini or regular cherry tomatoes

2 tbsp picked oregano leaves

salt and black pepper

1. Put the sliced garlic and 3 tablespoons of oil into a small frying pan and place it on a medium heat. Cook for about 8 minutes, or until the garlic turns lightly golden. Strain the oil through a small sieve set over a bowl, and set both the garlic and oil aside separately.

2. Use a box grater to roughly grate the plum tomatoes (p. 88), discarding the skins. Drain the grated tomato in a sieve set over a bowl and leave for about 5 minutes – you want about 400g of grated tomato pulp. Discard (or drink) the drained tomato liquid, then put the grated tomato into the bowl and stir in the crushed garlic, chilli flakes, vinegar, the remaining 2 tablespoons of oil, ¾ teaspoon of salt and a good grind of pepper.

3. Place a well-greased griddle pan on a high heat. Brush both sides of the ciabatta slices with a little olive oil to coat and, once the pan is hot, grill for about 90 seconds per side, or until nicely grilled and toasty. Do this in about two batches. Next, grill the cherry tomatoes until nicely charred and only just starting to burst a little, about 5 minutes.

4. Place the bread slices so that they're nestled together on a plate and spoon over the grated tomato mixture. Top with the grilled cherry tomatoes and the fried garlic and its oil, then sprinkle with the oregano. Serve right away.

Make it your own:
– Use other breads (such as focaccia or sourdough) and other fresh herbs that need using up.

_____

_____

_____

On grating tomatoes

If you've cooked through an Ottolenghi recipe (or three), you might have noticed that it's not uncommon for our recipes to call upon 'grating tomatoes'. In return, we almost always get asked, but how do you even grate a tomato?

If it's not a technique you're familiar with, then we're here to tell you that grating tomatoes is the surest, fastest way to get all the juicy pulp and seeds – sans skin.

• To grate a tomato all you need is: a **box grater**, and a **wide bowl** to catch the pulp and juice. You might also need a **sieve**, if you want to drain the pulp of any juice.

• Place the grater upright in your bowl and gently push your ripe tomatoes against the coarser side of the grater, and grate until you are left with just skin. Make sure to only go as far as you can (careful of your fingers!). The riper the tomato, the easier it will be to grate. Discard the skin.

• Once you've collected all your grated tomato goodness, you can then use it as a dip as we do for the za'atar parathas (p. 28), as a topping as in the grilled bread with tomato and fried garlic (p. 86), cooked into the base of soups and stews as in the magical chicken and Parmesan soup (p. 143) or simply stirred into dishes for freshness as we do in both the (one jar of) butter beans with preserved lemon, chilli and herb oil (p. 15) and the braised beef short ribs with butter beans and figs (p. 125).

Butternut squash with orange oil and burnt honey

Prep time: *15 minutes*
Cook time: *40 minutes*
Infusion time: *20 minutes to 1 hour*

This dish is one for the autumn months, the sunset shades of squash, orange and honey adding warmth to your table. Blitzing olive oil with orange peel is a quick way to infuse the oil used here without having to heat it up or wait very long. Trust us when we say that what makes this dish so memorable is the added details.

Serves 4, as a starter or side

1 **butternut squash** (*1.1kg*), *peeled, halved lengthways, deseeded and then cut into 1cm-thick half-moons (900g)*
2 tbsp olive oil
¼ tsp freshly grated nutmeg
1½ tbsp runny honey
1½ tsp cider vinegar
40g pecorino, *thinly sliced into ¼cm-thick shards*
1½ tbsp pickd oregano leaves, *with some stem attached*
20g pumpkin seeds, *toasted*
salt and black pepper

ORANGE-INFUSED OIL
2 oranges
45ml olive oil

1. Preheat the oven to 240°C fan or as high as your oven can go.

2. For the infused oil, finely shave the orange peel into strips, giving you 15g of peel (avoiding any pith). Roughly chop the peel, then transfer to the small bowl of a food processor. Add the oil and blitz for 1 minute, or until the peel is finely chopped. Transfer to a bowl and leave to infuse for 20–60 minutes. Strain through a sieve into a separate bowl, discarding the solids.

3. Segment both the peeled oranges; do this over a sieve set over a bowl to catch the juice. Set aside the segments and 1 tablespoon of the collected juice for the dressing.

4. Put the butternut squash, olive oil, nutmeg, ½ teaspoon of salt and a good grind of pepper into a large bowl, tossing to combine. Divide between two parchment-lined baking trays, spacing the pieces so that they're not overlapping, and bake for 20–25 minutes, turning the pieces halfway through, until cooked through and nicely browned. Set aside to cool to room temperature.

5. Meanwhile, put the honey into a small frying pan on a medium-high heat. Bring to the boil, then cook for 2–3 minutes, stirring occasionally, until the honey turns to a deep brown caramel. Remove from the heat and immediately stir in the orange segments, the 1 tablespoon of reserved juice and the vinegar. Set aside to cool slightly.

6. Arrange the butternut squash and pecorino on a large platter. Pour over the burnt honey dressing, and top with the oregano, pumpkin seeds and orange oil.

Make it your own:
- Double or triple the amount of orange oil and keep it in a sealed jar for drizzling over salads, roasted vegetables or fruit and yoghurt.
- Swap out the butternut squash for its other orange friend, the pumpkin.

_____
_____
_____

Lime and poppy seed slaw with curry leaf oil

Prep time: *25 minutes*
Cook time: *40 minutes*

Eat this zingy slaw al fresco, with the spicy vindaloo photographed alongside (p. 110), though it's also just as great on its own. Doubling up the turmeric cashews won't hurt either; they're super-duper special and will keep for up to a week in a sealed container (though we doubt they'll last that long).

Serves 6, as a side

1 white cabbage *(850g), core removed and head finely shredded (700g)*

1–2 carrots *(180g), peeled, halved widthways, then thinly sliced and julienned*

1 red onion *(120g), halved and very thinly sliced*

15g picked fresh coriander leaves, *with some stem attached*

5g picked mint leaves

salt and black pepper

TURMERIC CASHEWS

2 tbsp light soft brown sugar

2½ tsp olive oil

¾ tsp ground turmeric

200g roasted and salted cashews

2 tsp cumin seeds

CURRY LEAF OIL

1 red chilli, *thinly sliced, seeds and all (10g)*

3 tbsp olive oil

20 fresh curry leaves *(from 2 sprigs)*

LIME DRESSING

70ml lime juice *(from about 4 limes)*

2 tsp Dijon mustard

2 garlic cloves, *crushed*

1 tbsp poppy seeds

¼ tsp salt

75ml olive oil

1. Preheat the oven to 160°C fan. Line a medium baking tray with baking parchment.

2. Make the turmeric cashews. Put the sugar, oil, turmeric and 2 tablespoons of water into a small saucepan. Bring to the boil on a medium heat, stirring often, then add the cashews and cumin. Cook for another 3–4 minutes, stirring constantly, until the seeds and nuts are coated in a sticky glaze. Transfer to your prepared baking tray, using a spatula to spread the nuts out. Bake for 14 minutes, stirring once halfway, until golden. Set aside to cool completely.

3. Make the curry leaf oil by putting the chilli and oil into a small frying pan. Place it on a medium heat and cook for 7 minutes, or until the chilli starts to develop a shine, then add the curry leaves and cook for 2–3 minutes more, stirring often, until the leaves turn translucent. Transfer to a bowl and set aside.

4. Make the dressing by putting the lime juice, mustard, garlic, poppy seeds and ¼ teaspoon of salt into a small bowl and whisking to combine. Slowly drizzle in the olive oil, whisking continuously until incorporated.

5. In a large bowl, combine the cabbage, carrots, onion, ½ teaspoon of salt and a good grind of pepper. Pour over the dressing, mixing well to combine, and leave to soften slightly, about 15 minutes. Fold in the herbs, then transfer to a large serving platter. Drizzle the curry leaf oil all over and sprinkle with a handful of the turmeric cashews, serving the rest in a bowl alongside, to munch on.

Make it your own:

– Play with your nuts. Blanched peanuts or almonds would work just as well here!
– Make the slaw with different cabbages, kohlrabi and other crunchy veggies.

Fennel and courgette salad with preserved lemon dressing

Prep time: *35 minutes*
Cook time: *15 minutes*

Every so often, the team will put their heads together and brainstorm recipe ideas. Gitai, listening intently while tapping away at his computer, will let out the occasional murmur of agreement, sigh of disapproval or chip in with his suggestions. We often joke that 'fennel salad' is Gitai's signature go-to, his love of raw vegetables so very compelling. This salad is dedicated wholeheartedly to Gitai, who has contributed plenty of inspired ideas to the recipes developed at the OTK.

Serve this on a hot summer's day, alongside a summery spread and a chilled glass of wine. You can make the dressing well in advance, but don't mix everything together until just before serving; it releases water as it sits.

Serves 4, as a side

20g mint leaves, *roughly chopped*

20g dill, *roughly chopped*

25g chives, *roughly cut into 2cm lengths*

75ml olive oil

2 large fennel bulbs *(750g), trimmed, halved lengthways and finely shaved on a mandolin or by hand*

2 courgettes *(420g), trimmed and finely shaved into strips on a mandolin or by hand*

1 tbsp lemon juice

1½ tsp fennel seeds, *toasted and roughly crushed with a pestle and mortar*

1½ tsp pink peppercorns, *roughly crushed with a pestle and mortar*

salt and black pepper

PRESERVED LEMON DRESSING

40g preserved lemon *(1–2 lemons), pips discarded and flesh and skin roughly chopped (35g)*

½ small shallot, *roughly chopped (20g)*

1 garlic clove, *crushed*

1½ tbsp lemon juice

2½ tbsp olive oil

1. Make the dressing by putting the preserved lemon, shallot, garlic and lemon juice into the small bowl of a food processor and blitzing until finely chopped. With the machine running, gradually add the oil and blitz for 1–2 minutes more, until completely smooth. Transfer to a small bowl.

2. Put all the herbs, 4 tablespoons of oil and a pinch each of salt and pepper into the food processor and pulse to finely chop.

3. Add the fennel, courgette, lemon juice, ⅔ teaspoon of salt and a good grind of pepper to a large bowl and mix well to combine. Set aside for 5 minutes to soften, then add the herb mixture and toss together well.

4. Transfer half the salad to a large plate, and spoon over half the dressing and half the fennel seeds and pink peppercorns. Repeat once more, drizzle with the last tablespoon of oil and serve right away.

Grilled confit parsnips with herbs and vinegar

Prep time: *20 minutes*
Cook time: *1 hour 20 minutes*

Good old parsnips, the most underrated of root vegetables, making their appearance on the odd occasion but not nearly enough. Here they are given some extra love and attention: first by letting them cook slowly and gently in oil, then by grilling them for that smoky hit. Save the flavourful oil that you're left with – use it to dress salads or to drizzle over dips or mezze.

Serves 4–6, as a side

2 red chillies, *thinly sliced at a slight angle (20g), deseeded if you don't like heat*

3 tbsp apple cider vinegar

750g medium parsnips, *peeled and halved lengthways*

11 garlic cloves, *peeled, 10 left whole and 1 crushed*

450ml olive oil

15g fresh coriander, *roughly chopped*

10g parsley, *roughly chopped*

1 tsp ground allspice

flaked sea salt and black pepper

1. Preheat the oven to 160°C fan. Put the chillies, vinegar and a small pinch of flaked salt into a medium bowl. Leave to pickle lightly.

2. Put the parsnips, 10 whole garlic cloves, oil and 1 tablespoon of flaked salt into a high-sided baking dish about 30cm x 20cm in size. Cover tightly with foil, then transfer to the oven to bake for 1 hour, or until a knife slides easily into the thicker part of the parsnips. Remove the parsnips and garlic, reserving the oil.

3. Place a well-greased griddle pan on a high heat and ventilate your kitchen well. Once hot, grill the parsnips in 2–3 batches, until deeply charred on both sides, about 2–3 minutes per batch. Transfer to a large bowl (or dish) while you continue with the rest. Grill the garlic cloves for a minute until charred, then transfer to the bowl of parsnips.

4. Put the herbs, crushed garlic, 60ml of the reserved parsnip oil, ¼ teaspoon of flaked salt and a good grind of pepper into the small bowl of a food processor and blitz until finely chopped.

5. Add the herb mixture, pickled chillies and allspice to the parsnip bowl, tossing gently to combine, then transfer to a large serving platter. Drizzle with 2 more tablespoons of the parsnip oil and serve warm or at room temperature.

Make it your own:
- Skip the grilling and roast the confit parsnips in a hot oven until nicely coloured.
- Try this technique with other root vegetables, such as potatoes or turnips, adjusting the cooking times as necessary.

_____

_____

_____

Brussels sprout and Parmesan salad with lemon dressing

Prep time: *25 minutes*
Cook time: *35 minutes*

We would encourage you to eat your brussels with plenty of texture (well roasted or raw) and coated in punchy flavours, such as salty Parmesan, umami anchovies and spicy mustard. Serve this salad as a side to a Sunday roast or do what we did and eat it alongside the cheesy polenta and tomato sauce (p. 24).

Serves 4, as a side

700g small brussels sprouts, *trimmed, 500g left whole and 200g thinly shaved on a mandolin or by hand*

120ml olive oil, *plus extra for drizzling*

60ml lemon juice

3 garlic cloves, *crushed*

1½ tbsp wholegrain mustard

2 anchovies in oil, *drained and roughly chopped*

60g Parmesan, *20g roughly grated and the rest cut into thin shards*

120g kale leaves, *stems discarded and leaves thinly shredded (100g)*

1 small red onion, *halved and thinly sliced (80g)*

20g picked basil leaves

70g blanched hazelnuts, *well toasted and very roughly chopped*

salt and black pepper

1. Preheat the oven to 220°C fan.

2. Put the whole brussels sprouts, 2 tablespoons of oil, ½ teaspoon of salt and a good grind of pepper on a parchment-lined baking tray and mix to combine. Roast for 18 minutes, stirring halfway, until well browned and cooked through. Leave to cool.

3. Meanwhile, make the dressing by putting the lemon juice, garlic, mustard, anchovies, grated Parmesan, the remaining 90ml of oil, ¼ teaspoon of salt and a good grind of pepper into the small bowl of a food processor and blitzing until smooth.

4. Put the kale, the thinly shaved raw brussels sprouts, the dressing, ¼ teaspoon of salt and a good grind of pepper into a large mixing bowl and toss together well, massaging the leaves a little. Leave to soften and wilt slightly, about 10 minutes.

5. To the bowl add the onion, basil, chopped hazelnuts, Parmesan shards and roasted brussels sprouts and mix to combine. Pile into a large serving dish.

Make it your own:
- Lose the fish: swap out the anchovies for capers.
- Use other cabbage, such as hispi cabbage, instead of brussels sprouts.

Who
does
the

Dishes
Dishes
Dishes
Dishes
Dishes
Dishes
Dishes
Dishes
Dishes
Dishes
Dishes
Dishes
Dishes

Who does the dishes

There's a point during the day – around late afternoon – once our trials have been tested and tasted, our recipes modified and tweaked, when the dish area starts to look a little too full, the plates piled a little too high and the sink a little too ready to be soaped down. It's at this point that one-pan dishes are a welcome addition to our repertoire, but this chapter isn't really about the washing-up (although fewer dishes is always an added bonus).

Who does the dishes is all about cooking things in one pan, one tray, one dish – a single vessel for all the ingredients to hang out in, get to know one another and then, once they're comfortable, to soften and let their guard down. Eventually, and as they cook down, the individual ingredients begin to give a little – releasing their unique properties unto each other and morphing into their collective purpose. This character-building softens their cores and hardens their exteriors, forming golden shades of delicious personality. At times they'll need a little bit of help to get them going – a stir, a nudge, a 180° turn – but you can mostly leave them to their own devices.

The confit tandoori chickpeas (p. 105) is perhaps our best example of a one-pan dish with 'minimal effort, maximum oomph'. Our favourite little bean comes together with its animated friends – ginger, garlic, spices! – and, given the right environment, transforms into an intensely flavoured dish to be mopped up with bread or rice or simply dug into with a spoon (and an appetite). The 5-a-day toad-in-the-hole (p. 106) needs a little more maintenance, a delicate balance of timing and temperature, but is worth it for the end result of puffed-up, crispy batter and soft, beetroot-stained root veggies.

We've included this chapter in the book for several reasons, the most important of all being that, of all the recipes out there, one-tray bakes get the majority vote in many a popularity contest. The second being that a 'raid your shelves' book can only be improved with a 'then throw it into a pot' instruction. Love your shelves, but also love that there's a lot less washing-up too!

Confit tandoori chickpeas

Prep time: *25 minutes*
Cook time: *1 hour
20 minutes*

These chickpeas have had their fair share of Insta fame for a multitude of reasons. The first being that the simplicity of the dish makes it really quite attractive: throw everything into a pan and pop it into the oven, leaving it to its own devices (and you to yours). The second being that slow-cooking the chickpeas in oil without added liquid makes them super soft, allowing all the aromatics to break down into the oil. Lastly, this dish can easily be made ahead and served later; it only improves with time. Swap out Greek yoghurt with a non-dairy alternative for a completely vegan meal, and serve with rice.

Serves 4

2 tins of chickpeas
   (800g), drained (480g)

11 garlic cloves, *peeled,
   10 left whole and 1 crushed*

30g fresh ginger, *peeled and
   julienned*

**400g datterini or regular
   cherry tomatoes**

3 red chillies, *mild or spicy,
   a slit cut down their length*

1 tbsp tomato paste

2 tsp cumin seeds, *roughly
   crushed with a pestle and
   mortar*

2 tsp coriander seeds,
   *roughly crushed with
   a pestle and mortar*

½ tsp ground turmeric

½ tsp chilli flakes

**2 tsp red Kashmiri chilli
   powder**

1 tsp caster sugar

200ml olive oil

180g Greek-style yoghurt

15g picked mint leaves

30g fresh coriander, *roughly
   chopped*

2–3 limes: *juiced to get 1 tbsp
   and the rest cut into wedges
   to serve*

salt

1. Preheat the oven to 150°C fan.

2. Put the chickpeas, whole garlic cloves, ginger, tomatoes, chillies, tomato paste, spices, sugar, oil and 1 teaspoon of salt into a large sauté pan, for which you have a lid, and mix everything together to combine. Cover with the lid, transfer to the oven and cook for 75 minutes, stirring halfway through, until the aromatics have softened and the tomatoes have nicely broken down.

3. Meanwhile, put the yoghurt, mint, fresh coriander, lime juice, crushed garlic and ¼ teaspoon of salt into a food processor and blitz until smooth and the herbs are finely chopped.

4. Serve the chickpeas directly from the pan, with the yoghurt and lime wedges alongside.

Make it your own:
   – Jarred butter beans would be great here! A simple gram for gram swap.
   – No Kashmiri chilli powder? Use an equal amount of paprika instead.

5-a-day toad-in-the-hole

Prep time: *30 minutes*
Cook time: *1 hour 40 minutes*
Resting time: *30 minutes*

This vegetarian take on the classic dish features five different vegetables, which, in our terms, counts towards the prerequisite five-a-day. The trick here is to get the oil very hot before pouring in the batter, working very quickly to get it back into the oven as soon as possible – allowing for the batter to rise and puff up as it should. Making your own gravy means using a few more dishes, but we think it is truly worth it.

Serves 4–6

BATTER

4 large eggs

350ml whole milk

2 tbsp English mustard

230g plain flour, *sifted*

1 tsp salt

4 tbsp sunflower oil

FILLING

½ large celeriac *(480g),*
peeled and cut into 6 wedges
(450g)

350g beetroot *(about 2),*
peeled and each cut into
8 wedges (300g)

½ large swede *(350g), peeled*
and cut into 12 wedges (320g)

75ml olive oil

2 tbsp tomato paste

2 tbsp maple syrup

200g datterini or regular
cherry tomatoes, *left whole*

2 rosemary sprigs

salt and black pepper

MUSHROOM GRAVY
(OPTIONAL)

30g dried porcini
mushrooms

800ml boiling water

2 tbsp olive oil

1 large onion, *finely chopped*
(220g)

3 garlic cloves, *crushed*

1 tbsp tomato paste

1 tbsp finely chopped
rosemary leaves

2½ tbsp plain flour

1 tbsp balsamic vinegar

5g chives, *sliced into 1cm*
lengths

1. Preheat the oven to 200°C fan.

2. Put the dried mushrooms and boiling water into a heatproof bowl. Cover with a plate and let them steep for at least 20 minutes.

3. Make the batter by putting the eggs, milk and mustard into a large bowl and whisking vigorously until foamy, about a minute. Put the flour and salt into a separate large bowl, then pour in the egg mixture. Whisk until smooth and no lumps remain. Set aside for 30 minutes.

4. Put all the root vegetables, the olive oil, tomato paste, ¾ teaspoon of salt and a good grind of pepper into a large roasting tin, roughly 34cm x 26 cm. Roast for 20 minutes, then stir in the maple syrup. Return to the oven for 15 minutes more, until softened and nicely coloured. Transfer the vegetables and flavourful oil to a bowl and give the roasting tin a good rinse and dry.

5. Add the sunflower oil to the wiped-out roasting tin and place in the oven for 6 minutes, to heat up. Working quickly and very carefully, remove the hot tin from the oven and pour in the batter. Top evenly with the roasted vegetables and their oil, the cherry tomatoes and the rosemary sprigs. Return to the oven for 20 minutes, then lower the heat to 180°C fan and cook for 25 minutes more.

6. Meanwhile, make the gravy. Heat the oil in a medium saucepan on a medium-high heat, then add the onion and cook for 7 minutes, stirring occasionally, until softened and browned. Add the garlic, tomato paste and rosemary and cook for a minute more. Add the flour, stirring to coat, then slowly pour in the steeped porcini mushrooms and their liquid, stirring constantly to avoid lumps. Add 1 teaspoon of salt and a generous grind of pepper and bring to a simmer. Lower the heat to medium and cook for 12 minutes, then add the vinegar and cook for 5 minutes more, or until thickened to a gravy. Keep warm until ready to serve.

7. Stir two-thirds of the chives into the gravy and sprinkle the rest over the toad-in-the-hole. Serve warm, with the gravy to pour alongside.

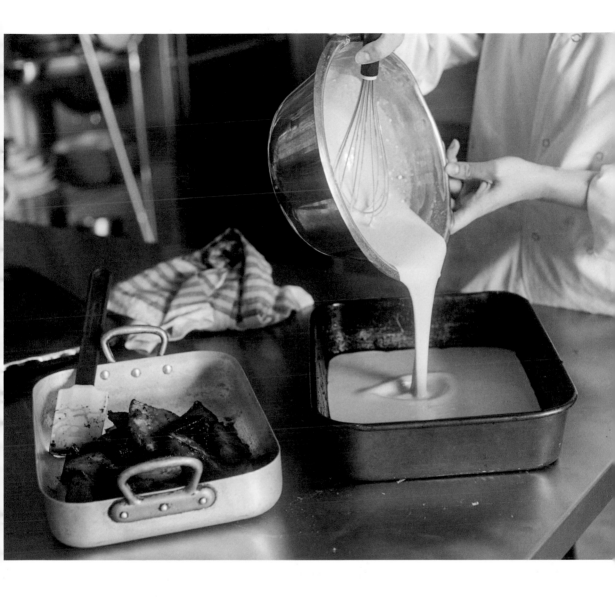

Make it your own:
- Feel free to use a shop-bought gravy to save time (and washing-up).
- Use more or less of your favourite root vegetables.

_____

_____

_____

Spicy pulled pork vindaloo

Prep time: *20 minutes*
Cook time: *6 hours*
15 minutes

When feeding a crowd, we are huge fans of large cuts of meat or large whole vegetables, slow-cooked with minimal work and maximum flavour. The most work involved here is making the vindaloo paste, a small ask for a dish that packs a serious kick. Serve this pork with the lime and poppy seed slaw with curry leaf oil (p. 92), or with a good-quality shop-bought slaw.

Serves 8

3 cinnamon sticks,
   roughly broken
15 cardamom pods
1½ tsp black peppercorns
10 dried Kashmiri chillies,
   stems removed
1½ tbsp cumin seeds
2 tsp black mustard seeds
¼ tsp ground cloves
10 garlic cloves, *peeled*
50g fresh ginger, *peeled and*
   roughly chopped
1 tbsp caster sugar
2 tbsp tomato paste
90ml apple cider vinegar
150ml full-fat coconut milk
2.2kg pork shoulder, *rolled*
   and boneless
3 tbsp sunflower oil
3 onions, *roughly chopped*
   (450g)
20g fresh coriander,
   roughly chopped
2 tbsp lime juice
salt and black pepper

TO SERVE
500g Greek-style yoghurt
120g mango chutney,
   store-bought
8 white soft bread rolls,
   store-bought

1. Put the first 13 ingredients into a medium bowl and mix to combine. Leave to soak for 30 minutes, then transfer to a food processor or blender and blitz until smooth, about 3–4 minutes.

2. Preheat the oven to 150°C fan.

3. Pat dry the pork, then sprinkle all over with 1 teaspoon of salt. Put 2 tablespoons of oil into a large, heavy-based cast-iron saucepan, for which you have a lid, on a medium-high heat. Add the pork and sear to lightly brown on all sides, about 8 minutes. Remove the pork and set aside. Add the remaining tablespoon of oil and the onions, stirring to lightly colour, about 3 minutes, then add the blitzed spice mixture, 450ml of water and

1 teaspoon of salt. Return the pork to the pan, bring to the boil, then cover with the lid and transfer to the oven to bake for 4 hours, basting every hour or so. Remove the lid and return to the oven for 80 minutes more, basting once or twice throughout, until browned and the sauce is thick and rich.

4. Use two forks to shred the pork directly in the pan with all its juices. You can choose to shred the skin as well, or discard it. Stir in the coriander and lime juice.

5. Place the yoghurt in a small bowl and swirl through the chutney. Serve this and the bread rolls alongside the pork, building your own plate or sandwich as you please.

Get ahead:
 – Make the whole thing
   the day before you want
   to serve it, reheating
   the pulled pork on the
   stovetop.

Make it your own:
- Not into heat? Use half the amount of chilli asked for.
- Use any dried mild red chilli in place of dried Kashmiri chillies.
- Swap out the pork for rolled boneless lamb shoulder, keeping an eye on cooking times.

_____

_____

113

Baked orzo puttanesca

Prep time: *15 minutes*
Cook time: *50 minutes*

This is a one-pot meal in its own right, but also a bit of a kitchen raid, using up tins, jars and packets from your cupboards and a few bits from the fridge as well.

Serves 4

60ml olive oil

1 onion, *finely chopped (150g)*

6 garlic cloves, *crushed*

½ tsp chilli flakes

3 anchovies in oil, *drained and roughly chopped (12g)*

2 tbsp capers

30g preserved lemon, *inner parts discarded and skin thinly sliced into strips (12g)*

70g pitted Kalamata olives, *roughly torn in half*

2 tins of good-quality tuna in olive oil *(320g), drained and roughly flaked*

1 tbsp tomato paste

1 tin of chopped tomatoes *(400g)*

250g dried orzo

1–2 plum tomatoes *(180g), cored and cut into ½cm-thick rounds*

40g Parmesan, *finely grated*

5g picked basil leaves, *roughly torn*

salt and black pepper

1. Preheat the oven to 200°C fan.

2. Put 3 tablespoons of oil into a large ovenproof sauté pan, for which you have a lid, on a medium-high heat. Add the onion and cook for 8 minutes, stirring occasionally, until softened and browned. Add the garlic, chilli and anchovies and cook for 1 minute more, until fragrant. Stir in the capers, half the preserved lemon, 45g of olives, the tuna, tomato paste, tinned tomatoes, orzo, 450ml of water, 1 teaspoon of salt and a generous grind of pepper. Bring to a simmer, then cover with the lid and bake for 20 minutes, until the orzo is cooked through.

3. Turn the oven temperature up to 230°C fan. Remove the lid, top with the sliced tomatoes, sprinkle over the cheese and bake for 10–12 minutes more, until lightly browned. Leave to sit for 10 minutes.

4. Top with the remaining olives and preserved lemon, the basil leaves and the remaining tablespoon of oil.

Make it your own:

– Lose the fish: swap out the tinned tuna for jarred artichoke hearts and the anchovies for more capers.

_____

_____

_____

_____

_____

Berbere spiced chicken, carrots and chickpeas

Prep time: *25 minutes*
Cook time: *1 hour 25 minutes*

Berbere is an Ethiopian spice blend with quite a bit of a kick, so use a little less if you're not into heat. We use store-bought berbere spice, but you can also toast and grind your own homemade blend, especially if you have a well-stocked spice rack. We love this for being a complete meal in a tray, but wouldn't say no to a big ol' bowl of greens to eat alongside.

Serves 4–6

1 large onion, *roughly chopped (220g)*

6 garlic cloves, *peeled*

45g fresh coriander, *stalks (25g) and leaves (20g) separated and roughly chopped*

2½ tbsp berbere spice *(we recommend the Bart brand)*

2 tbsp tomato paste

2½ tbsp runny honey, *plus a little extra for drizzling*

3 tbsp apple cider vinegar

90ml olive oil

800g carrots, *peeled and cut into 4–5cm lengths (680g)*

2 tins of chickpeas *(800g), drained (480g)*

8 medium chicken thighs, *skin on and bone in*

2–3 oranges: *1 left whole and the rest juiced to get 100ml*

salt and black pepper

1. Preheat the oven to 200°C fan.

2. Put the onion, garlic, coriander stalks, berbere spice, tomato paste, honey, 1 tablespoon of vinegar, 4 tablespoons of oil, 1¾ teaspoons of salt and a good grind of black pepper into a food processor and blitz to a smooth paste.

3. Put the blitzed onion mixture, carrots, chickpeas, chicken, orange juice and 150ml of water into a large roasting tin, roughly 34cm x 26cm in size, and toss everything together to combine. Arrange the thighs so that they're skin side up and slightly nestled on top, then cover the dish tightly with foil and bake for 30 minutes. Remove the foil and return to the oven for 40 minutes more, rotating the tin halfway through, or until everything is cooked through and nicely coloured. Set aside to settle slightly, about 10 minutes.

4. Meanwhile, peel and segment the whole orange and then roughly chop the flesh. Put this into a medium bowl along with the chopped coriander leaves, the remaining 2 tablespoons of vinegar, the remaining 2 tablespoons of oil and a pinch each of salt and pepper, and mix to combine.

5. When ready to serve, spoon the coriander salsa all over the top and serve directly from the roasting tin.

Make it your own:

– Swap out the berbere spice for other spice blends such as hawaij (p. 16).
– Use other chicken segments if you prefer.

_____

_____

Za'atar salmon and tahini

Prep time: *5 minutes*
Cook time: *20 minutes*

If you haven't yet paired fish with tahini, then you're in for a real treat. This version combines tahini with herbaceous za'atar and sour sumac, our ever familiar but much treasured test kitchen staples. We strongly recommend using creamy, nutty tahini that's sourced from countries within the Levant. Eat this shortly after cooking, as cooked tahini doesn't sit or reheat very well.

Serves 4

4 salmon fillets *(600g), skin on and pin bones removed*

2 tbsp za'atar

2 tsp sumac, *plus ½ tsp extra for sprinkling*

60ml olive oil

250g baby spinach

90g tahini

3 garlic cloves, *crushed*

3½ tbsp lemon juice

1½ tbsp roughly chopped coriander leaves

salt and black pepper

1. Preheat the oven to 220°C fan.

2. Pat dry the salmon and sprinkle with salt and pepper. In a small bowl, combine the za'atar and sumac, then sprinkle this all over the top of the salmon to create a crust.

3. Place a large ovenproof sauté pan on a medium-high heat and add a tablespoon of oil. Once hot, add the spinach and a pinch each of salt and pepper and cook for 2–3 minutes, until just wilted.

4. Top with the salmon, skin side down, and drizzle the top of the fish with 2 tablespoons of oil. Bake for 5 minutes.

5. Meanwhile, in a small bowl whisk together the tahini, garlic, 2½ tablespoons of lemon juice, a good pinch of salt and 100ml of water until smooth and quite runny.

6. When ready, remove the pan from the oven and pour the tahini all around the salmon (but not on the fish at all). Bake for another 5 minutes, or until the fish is cooked through and the tahini is bubbling. Spoon over the remaining tablespoon each of lemon juice and oil and top with the coriander and extra sumac.

Make it your own:
– Swap out the salmon for other sustainably caught fish, adjusting cooking times where needed.
– Use other leafy greens in place of spinach, such as kale or chard.

_____

_____

_____

_____

Chickpeas cacio e pepe

Prep time: *20 minutes*
Cook time: *2 hours*
10 minutes
Soaking time: *overnight*

These chickpeas are inspired by cacio e pepe, a rich Italian dish of pasta coated in lavish amounts of butter, black pepper and cheese. This uses a similar technique applied to our favourite little bean, using the flavourful Parmesan chickpea water to create the emulsified sauce. Chickpeas differ in size depending on where you are in the world, so if you feel that this should be a little looser, just add a splash of water. Be sure to start the night before by soaking your chickpeas.

Serves 4

300g dried chickpeas, *soaked overnight in plenty of water and 1 tsp bicarbonate of soda*
3 tbsp olive oil
8 garlic cloves, *crushed*
80g Parmesan, *finely grated, plus 1–2 optional Parmesan rinds (60g)*
¼ tsp bicarbonate of soda
2 red chillies, *thinly sliced into rounds, seeds and all*
2 tbsp apple cider vinegar
250g baby spinach
15g parsley, *roughly chopped*
100g unsalted butter, *fridge cold and cut into 2cm cubes*
salt and black pepper

1. Preheat the oven to 160°C fan.

2. Drain the chickpeas well and set them aside. Put 2 tablespoons of oil into a large, high-sided ovenproof sauté pan or cast-iron saucepan, for which you have a lid, and place on a medium-high heat. Once hot, add the garlic and cook for 90 seconds, until starting to colour. Add the Parmesan rinds, if using, the drained chickpeas, bicarbonate of soda, 1.2 litres of water and a very generous amount of coarsely cracked black pepper (give it about 40 grinds). Bring to the boil, skimming the scum from the surface as needed, then cover with the lid and bake in the oven for 75 minutes. Add ¾ teaspoon of salt and continue cooking, covered, for another 30 minutes, or until the chickpeas are very soft and the liquid has reduced by about half.

3. Meanwhile, mix together the chillies, vinegar and a small pinch of salt in a small bowl. Set aside to pickle.

4. Towards the last 10 minutes of cooking the chickpeas, put the last tablespoon of oil into a large frying pan on a medium-high heat and, once hot, cook the spinach, adding it to the pan in batches with ¼ teaspoon of salt until just wilted, about 4 minutes. Add the parsley and remove from the heat.

5. When the chickpeas are ready, remove the lid and, while still hot from the oven but off the heat, add a quarter of the butter cubes and about 15g of grated Parmesan, mixing until the butter has melted into the sauce. Continue in this way, adding a quarter more of the butter and 15g more of Parmesan until you've used up all 100g of butter and 60g of cheese. Finally, add another very generous grind of coarsely ground black pepper. The sauce will have thickened significantly, coating the chickpeas nicely. Add a splash more water if you like it looser. Remove the Parmesan rinds, if using.

6. Top with the spinach mixture, the pickled chillies and their liquid and a final sprinkling of Parmesan, serving any extra grated Parmesan alongside.

Make it your own:

– Swap out the pickled chillies for a squeeze of lemon instead.
– Serve with any greens, such as chard or broccolini.
– Use cannellini or butter beans, adjusting liquid levels.

_____

_____

_____

One-pan crispy spaghetti and chicken

Prep time: *30 minutes*
Cook time: *1 hour*

Yotam tested this dish out on his two little ones, the most brutally honest of critics, who were so keen that they asked for it two nights in a row – a true testament to midweek dinner success. To top this off, it is easy to prepare and fun to eat and doesn't call upon any hard-to-source ingredients. Cooking the spaghetti in this way lends plenty of texture, allowing for crispier bits around the edges and softer bits throughout.

Serves 4

2 tbsp olive oil

6 chicken thighs, *skin on and bone in (700g)*

1 large onion, *cut into 1cm dice (220g)*

4 garlic cloves, *crushed*

2 tbsp picked thyme leaves

3 tbsp tomato paste

250g dried spaghetti, *broken into thirds*

20g Parmesan, *finely grated*

20g fresh breadcrumbs, *finely blitzed*

10g parsley, *finely chopped*

1½ tsp finely grated lemon zest

salt and black pepper

1. Preheat the oven to 200°C fan.

2. Put 1 tablespoon of oil into a large, ovenproof sauté pan, for which you have a lid, and place on a high heat. Season the chicken with ¾ teaspoon of salt and plenty of pepper and add to the hot oil, skin side down. Leave for 7 minutes, without turning over, to brown well.

3. Turn the heat down to medium-high, then add the onion and stir, turning the chicken over. Cook for 5 minutes, until the onion has softened and is lightly browned. Add the garlic, 1 tablespoon of thyme and all the tomato paste and cook, stirring, for 1 minute more. Arrange the chicken skin side up, add 150ml of water and cook for 10 minutes, stirring occasionally, until most of the liquid has reduced. Add another 450ml of water, ½ teaspoon of salt and a good grind of pepper, then add the spaghetti, stirring to submerge and evenly distribute it. Use tongs to lift the chicken pieces so that they sit on top of the spaghetti, skin side up. Bring to a simmer, cover with the lid and bake in the oven for 30 minutes, at which stage all the liquid should have been absorbed.

4. Meanwhile, in a small bowl mix together the Parmesan, breadcrumbs, parsley, lemon zest and the remaining tablespoon of thyme.

5. After 30 minutes in the oven, remove the pasta pan and reset the oven to a high grill setting. Sprinkle the breadcrumb mix over the pasta and chicken, drizzle with the remaining oil, and grill for 3–4 minutes, until nicely browned and crisp. Leave to settle for 5 minutes before serving warm, directly from the pan.

Make it your own:
 – Use up any soft herbs or hard cheeses you have on hand.
 – Add some spice and chilli heat if making an adult version.

_____

_____

_____

Make it your own:
- Use cannellini or white kidney beans in place of the butter beans if you like.
- We like the combination of sweet spices here, but feel free to play around with what you have in your cupboards.

Braised beef short ribs with butter beans and figs

Prep time: *25 minutes*
Cook time: *4 hours 10 minutes*

This is a braise for the winter months, when fall-off-the-bone ribs and warming spices are what you're craving. Don't be intimidated by the long cooking time here – it's mostly a waiting game once the pot goes into the oven, so it can easily be put together in the afternoon, ready for a decadent dinner.

Serves 4

2 onions, *roughly chopped (300g)*

6 garlic cloves, *peeled*

4cm piece of fresh ginger, *peeled and roughly chopped (40g)*

2 green chillies, *roughly chopped, seeds and all (30g)*

6 beef short ribs *(1.5kg)*

60ml olive oil

4 whole star anise

10 cardamom pods, *roughly bashed open with a pestle and mortar*

1½ tbsp tomato paste

2 tsp ground allspice

2 tsp ground cumin

5–6 large plum tomatoes *(600g), two-thirds roughly chopped (400g) and the rest roughly grated (p. 88) and skins discarded*

100g soft dried figs, *roughly chopped into 1½cm pieces*

1 jar of butter beans *(700g), drained (550g)*

30g chives, *very finely chopped*

1½ tbsp lemon juice

300g large-leaf spinach, *stems discarded and leaves roughly torn (130g)*

salt and black pepper

1. Preheat the oven to 165°C fan.

2. Put the onions, garlic, ginger and chillies into a food processor, pulse until very finely chopped.

3. Pat dry the short ribs and lightly sprinkle them all over with salt and pepper. Put 2 tablespoons of oil into a large cast-iron ovenproof saucepan, for which you have a lid, on a medium-high heat. Fry the short ribs in two batches until deeply golden on all sides, about 4 minutes per batch. Remove the ribs and set aside.

4. Add the onion mixture to the saucepan along with the star anise and cardamom, and cook for 5 minutes to soften, stirring occasionally. Add the tomato paste, ground spices, chopped tomatoes, 1½ teaspoons of salt and a good grind of pepper and cook for 4 minutes more, until the tomatoes start to break down. Add the short ribs and 1.1 litres of water, bring to the boil, then cover with the lid and transfer to the oven. Cook for 3 hours, stirring a few times throughout.

5. Add the figs and cook for 30 minutes more, or until the figs have softened and the meat is very tender.

6. Towards the last 20 minutes of cooking, heat the butter beans in a saucepan with enough water to cover and a pinch of salt. Gently simmer for about 15 minutes, then drain off the liquid. Stir through the chives, the remaining 2 tablespoons of oil, the lemon juice and a good grind of pepper.

7. When ready, remove the short ribs from the pan, gently tugging at the bones to pull them away from the meat; discard the bones and set the meat aside.

8. Heat the sauce and stir through the spinach leaves to wilt, about 3 minutes. Add the grated tomato and remove from the heat.

9. Spoon the sauce into a large shallow platter and top with the beans and beef.

Sweet spiced mushroom and rice pilaf

Prep time: *25 minutes*
Cook time: *1 hour
55 minutes*

This robust vegan main scores major points for its liberal use of warming spices and both fresh and dried mushrooms. It's really quite a festive dish, suitable for the cooler months, and would need nothing more than some lightly cooked greens to eat alongside, or the butternut squash with orange oil (p. 91), for a very happy spread.

Serves 4 as a main, or 6 as a side

1–2 dried ancho chillies *(15g), stems removed*

30g dried porcini mushrooms

500ml vegetable stock, *or chicken stock, if not vegan*

500g oyster mushrooms, *left whole*

500g large portobello mushrooms, *stems discarded, each mushroom roughly broken by hand into 6 chunks*

1 large onion, *halved and cut into ½cm-thick slices*

10 garlic cloves, *peeled*

3 cinnamon sticks

4 whole star anise

150g soft dried apricots *(the plump orange kind), quartered*

150ml olive oil

350g basmati rice, *washed until the water runs clear and drained well*

3 spring onions, *thinly sliced at an angle (45g)*

5g picked parsley leaves, *with some stem attached*

salt and black pepper

1. Preheat the oven to 220°C fan.

2. Put the ancho chillies into a heatproof bowl and pour over enough boiling water to cover. Rehydrate for 20 minutes, then drain off the soaking liquid (save it for another use) and roughly chop the chillies, seeds and all.

3. Meanwhile, put the dried mushrooms, stock, 350ml of water, 1¼ teaspoons of salt and a good grind of pepper into a medium saucepan on a medium-high heat. Bring to a simmer, then set aside.

4. Put the oyster and portobello mushrooms, onion, garlic, chopped chillies, whole spices, apricots, 120ml of oil, 1 teaspoon of salt and a good grind of pepper into a roasting tin about 34cm x 26cm in size. Give everything a good stir, then bake for 40 minutes, stirring halfway through, until well browned.

5. Remove from the oven and transfer about half the mixture to a medium bowl. Stir the rice into the remaining mixture in the roasting tin, and set aside.

6. Bring the porcini mixture back up to a simmer. Pour this over the rice mixture and, without stirring, cover the tin tightly with foil. Bake for 25 minutes, until the rice is cooked through. Leave to sit, covered, for 10 minutes. Remove the foil and gently mix everything together.

7. Add the spring onions, parsley and remaining 2 tablespoons of oil to the reserved mushroom mixture, stirring to combine. Spoon this over the rice and serve.

Make it your own:
– Play around with other types of foraged finds, breaking them up into large chunks to keep intact their naturally 'meaty' integrity.
– Use other dried chillies in place of the ancho, such as cascabel or chipotle.

Charred tomatoes, onions and peppers with feta and harissa pine nuts

Prep time: *30 minutes*
Cook time: *1 hour 15 minutes*

This lands somewhere between a sauce and a dip, great on its own with warm flatbreads but would work just as well spooned over pasta, rice or baked potatoes.

Serves 4

75ml olive oil

4 red onions, *each cut into 8 wedges (480g)*

2 green jalapeños, *stems discarded and flesh chopped into 1cm-thick rounds*

2 red peppers (300g), *stems and seeds discarded, and flesh cut into 3–4cm pieces*

1 head of garlic, *skin on and halved widthways*

1.5kg plum tomatoes, *peeled and roughly chopped*

20g fresh coriander, *roughly chopped, plus 1 tbsp extra chopped coriander to serve*

1 tbsp coriander seeds

120g datterini or regular cherry tomatoes, *left whole*

120g Greek feta, *roughly crumbled into large chunks*

25g pine nuts

1 tbsp rose harissa

salt

1. Preheat the oven to 240°C fan (or as high as your oven can go).

2. Put 2 tablespoons of oil, the onions, jalapeños, peppers and garlic into a large roasting tin about 34cm x 26cm in size and give everything a good stir. Roast for 25 minutes, stirring two or three times throughout, until softened and well charred.

3. Remove the garlic halves and use a small knife to remove the cloves, putting them back into the tin and discarding the papery skins. Add the plum tomatoes, fresh coriander, coriander seeds and 1¾ teaspoons of salt and use the back of a large spoon to mash everything together, breaking apart the garlic and chillies a little. Return to the oven for another 30–35 minutes, stirring two or three times throughout, or until the tomatoes have broken down and the mixture has thickened.

4. Remove the dish from the oven and set it to a high grill setting. Top with the datterini/cherry tomatoes and feta and drizzle over 1 tablespoon of oil. Grill for 10 minutes, or until the feta and datterini/cherry tomatoes have taken on some colour.

5. Meanwhile, put the remaining 2 tablespoons of oil into a small frying pan on a medium-high heat. Add the pine nuts and cook until golden, shaking the pan frequently, about 3 minutes. Add the harissa, stirring to combine, then remove from the heat.

6. To serve, spoon over the harissa pine nuts and sprinkle with the extra coriander.

Make it your own:
- Use any soft herb you have on hand.
- Swap out the pine nuts for toasted almonds or walnuts.
- Veganise it: leave out the feta; it's just as tasty without.

_____

_____

Sticky sweet and sour plums and sausages

Prep time: *25 minutes*
Cook time: *1 hour 35 minutes*

Here we celebrate plums in all their beautiful red glory. As they cook, they gently break down to create a sweet/sour sauce for the sausages and potatoes. Paired with sticky pomegranate molasses and sour sumac, you can't really go wrong. Try to source pomegranate molasses from a Middle Eastern grocery store; it should be quite sharp and tangy and not overly sweet.

Serves 4

5 red onions, *each cut into 6 wedges (750g)*

2 heads of garlic, *skin on and each halved widthways*

3 baking potatoes *(750g), skin on and each quartered lengthways*

120ml olive oil

750g red plums *(about 10), halved and pitted (600g)*

3 rosemary sprigs

8 pork sausages

3 tbsp apple cider vinegar

90g pomegranate molasses

50g soft light brown sugar

2 tbsp sumac

10g picked parsley leaves, *with some stem attached*

salt and black pepper

1. Preheat the oven to 180°C fan.

2. Put the onions, garlic, potatoes, 5 tablespoons of oil, 100ml of water, 1½ teaspoons of salt and a good grind of pepper into a large roasting tin roughly 40cm x 30cm in size. Toss everything together, then bake for 35 minutes, stirring halfway through, until the vegetables have softened and started to take on some colour and the water has evaporated.

3. Add the plums (cut side up) and the rosemary, then nestle in the sausages. In a medium bowl, whisk together the vinegar, molasses, sugar, 2 tablespoons of water, 1½ tablespoons of sumac, 2 tablespoons of oil, ½ teaspoon of salt and a good grind of pepper and pour this all over the mixture in the tin. Return to the oven for 40 minutes, carefully turning over the sausages halfway through. Turn the oven temperature up to 200°C fan and roast for 10 minutes more, or until everything is nicely browned, the plums have broken down and the sauce is bubbling and sticky.

4. Toss together the parsley, the remaining 1½ teaspoons of sumac and the remaining tablespoon of oil and dot this all over the sausage mixture. Serve warm, directly from the tray.

Make it your own:
– Use any kind of sausages you like here: duck or chicken would work well, as would vegetarian sausages.
– Swap out the potatoes for sweet potatoes.

_____

_____

Fridge

Raid

Fridge raid

There's a universal sweet spot by the fridge, a familiar space in which we've all stood, door ajar and locked into a staring match with the fridge's contents. It's existing in that limbo between yourself and the next meal, waiting for inspiration to strike until . . . you see it. Eggs, begging to be pancakes. Rice, waiting to be fried. Chicken, wanting to be soup. As far as recipe-origin stories go, it's not that different at the OTK really. Sure, sometimes we'll go in with a fixed idea, a structured plan of how said dish should turn out, but this isn't always the case. Needless to say, we've all had to learn (the hard way, actually) that things don't always work out how we visualise them, diversions are a big part of the learning curve and many accidents are, in fact, happy ones.

The recipes in this chapter, although born via fridge raid, all have one thing in common: they speak of comfort and familiarity. They are dishes that are relatable, things we know and love and foods we grew up eating. With all the potential of comfort that this chapter has to offer, we tried hard to strike the right balance here between edgy and homey – dishes you'd want to dig into and eat, while also escaping predictability: a riff on mac 'n' cheese (p. 140), a Persian version of meatballs in tomato sauce (p. 156) or a very magical magical chicken and Parmesan soup (p. 143).

We want you to find comfort in this fridge raid chapter – echoes of familiarity in even the most unfamiliar of times – but also in other recipes dotted elsewhere in the book, as we put little spins on well-loved dishes that will hopefully find a place on your table.

Kale pesto strata with Gruyère and mustard

Prep time: *20 minutes*
Cook time: *1 hour 30 minutes*
Chilling time: *4 hours to overnight*

We're all about this strata, or savoury bread pudding, as it's one to assemble a day ahead, ready to be popped into the oven when you're about an hour away from dinner. A lot less stress with little mess for when your guests are around, and a great one to have as a veggie main or as part of a brunch spread.

Serves 4–6

500g sourdough loaf, *ends discarded (but crusts intact) and loaf sliced into ½cm-thick slices*

75g kale leaves, *stems discarded and leaves roughly torn*

40g parsley, *roughly chopped*

15g oregano leaves

1 red chilli, *roughly chopped (20g), deseeded if you don't like heat*

1 large shallot, *roughly chopped into 6 wedges (75g)*

2 garlic cloves, *roughly chopped*

135ml olive oil, *plus extra for greasing*

50g Parmesan, *roughly grated*

60g Gruyère, *roughly grated*

3 eggs, *plus 3 yolks*

700ml whole milk

300ml double cream

1½ tbsp Dijon mustard

1½ tbsp roughly chopped capers

1½ tbsp cider vinegar

salt and black pepper

1. Preheat the oven to 160°C fan. Spread the bread on two baking trays and bake for 10 minutes, or until lightly toasted. Set aside to cool.

2. Grease a 30cm x 20cm baking dish that is at least 6cm deep.

3. Make the pesto. Put the kale, parsley, oregano, chilli, shallot and garlic into a food processor and pulse until finely chopped. Add 90ml of oil, ¾ teaspoon of salt and a good grind of pepper, and pulse to a coarse paste. Measure out 75g of the mixture and set aside.

4. Use the rest of the kale mixture to generously coat both sides of the toasted bread slices. Layer the bread in the baking dish at an angle, sprinkling both cheeses in between as you go, so that the pieces overlap a little.

5. In a medium bowl, whisk together the eggs, yolks, milk, cream, mustard, ¾ teaspoon of salt and a good grind of pepper. Pour this over the bread, cover the dish with a piece of baking parchment, then weigh everything down with another, heavy baking dish. Refrigerate for at least 4 hours or preferably overnight.

6. Remove the strata from the fridge about an hour before baking, removing the weight and baking parchment. Cover tightly with foil.

7. Preheat the oven to 180°C fan. Bake for 30 minutes, then remove the foil and bake for 25 minutes more, or until deeply golden and bubbling. Leave to cool for at least 15 minutes before serving.

8. Combine the reserved pesto with the capers, vinegar and the remaining 3 tablespoons of oil and spoon this all over the strata to serve.

Make it your own:

- Swap out the kale for spinach and the herbs for whatever you have on hand.
- Use a mixture of different cheeses – cheddar and pecorino would work well here!

_____

_____

_____

M.E. mac 'n' cheese with za'atar pesto

Prep time: *25 minutes*
Cook time: *30 minutes*

This recipe is a Middle Eastern take on a mac 'n' cheese thanks to the addition of cumin, a herbaceous za'atar pesto and crispy fried onions. Cooking the macaroni in the milk, as we do here, bypasses having to make a béchamel. The starches are released into the soon-to-be-cheesy sauce, making it velvety and rich without the need for the more traditional flour-butter 'roux'.

To make the crispy onions, finely slice a couple of onions into thin rounds and toss with 2 tablespoons of cornflour, then fry in hot vegetable oil in about three batches, for 4 minutes per batch, or until golden.

Serves 4–6

MAC 'N' CHEESE

300g dried cavatappi or fusilli pasta

600–700ml whole milk

65g unsalted butter, *cut into roughly 3cm cubes*

3 garlic cloves, *crushed*

⅛ tsp ground turmeric

1½ tsp cumin seeds, *toasted and roughly crushed with a pestle and mortar*

75ml double cream

150g mature cheddar, *roughly grated*

180g Greek feta, *roughly crumbled*

salt and black pepper

45g crispy onions or shallots, *store-bought or homemade (see intro), to serve*

ZA'ATAR PESTO

1 large lemon

3 tbsp za'atar

20g fresh coriander, *roughly chopped*

1 garlic clove, *roughly chopped*

40g pine nuts, *lightly toasted*

90ml olive oil

Get ahead:

– Make the mac 'n' cheese ahead of time if you like, adding a splash of water to thin out when reheating.

Make it your own:

– Play with different cheeses and spices.
– Use different pasta shapes like macaroni, adjusting liquid levels as necessary.

---

1. Put the pasta, 600ml of milk, 350ml of water, the butter, garlic, turmeric, 1 teaspoon of salt and a good grind of pepper into a large sauté pan on a medium-high heat. Bring to a simmer, then turn the heat down to medium and cook, stirring occasionally, for 10–14 minutes, or until the pasta is al dente and the sauce has thickened from the pasta starches (it will still be quite saucy). If using cavatappi, you might need to add the extra 100ml of milk at this stage depending on how saucy you like your mac 'n' cheese. Turn the heat down to low and stir through the cumin, cream and both cheeses until the cheddar is nicely melted.

2. While the pasta is cooking, make the pesto. Finely grate the lemon to give you 1½ teaspoons of zest. Then use a small, sharp knife to peel and segment the lemon and roughly chop the segments. Place in a bowl with the lemon zest and set aside. Put the za'atar, coriander, garlic, pine nuts, ⅛ teaspoon of salt, a good grind of pepper and half the oil into a food processor and pulse a few times until you have a coarse paste. Add to the chopped lemon in the bowl and stir in the remaining oil.

3. Transfer the mac 'n' cheese to a large serving platter with a lip or a shallow bowl, dot all over with the pesto, then top with the crispy onions.

Magical chicken and Parmesan soup with pappardelle

Prep time: *15 minutes*
Cook time: *2 hours 25 minutes*

There's an undivided, universal power to chicken soup that translates across all cultures and borders. This broth is basically liquid magic, but our guess is the Parmesan rind might have something to do with it.

Serves 4

1 whole chicken *(1.4kg)*

1 head of garlic, *skin on and halved widthways, plus 4 extra peeled cloves, crushed*

1 onion, *cut into 4 wedges*

2 tbsp olive oil

2 carrots, *peeled and roughly cut into 1½cm cubes (220g)*

3 sticks of celery, *sliced at an angle into roughly 1cm-thick slices (200g)*

3 bay leaves

1½ tbsp finely chopped thyme leaves

1 Parmesan wedge, *60g finely grated and rind reserved*

5 plum tomatoes, *coarsely grated (p. 88) and skins discarded (320g)*

2 tsp tomato paste

180g dried pappardelle nests

15g basil leaves, *finely shredded*

1 red chilli, *deseeded and finely chopped (10g)*

salt and black pepper

1. Put the chicken, head of garlic, onion, 2 litres of water and 2¼ teaspoons of salt into a large saucepan, for which you have a lid, and bring to the boil. Lower to a simmer on a medium-low heat and cook, covered, for 80 minutes, or until the chicken is tender.

2. Remove the chicken and, when cool, shred the meat into large pieces, discarding the skin, bones and cartilage. Set aside.

3. Strain the stock through a sieve placed over a medium saucepan, discarding the solids. You will need 1.7 litres, so save any extra for another use.

4. Heat the oil in a large saucepan on a medium-high heat. Add the carrots and celery and cook for 4 minutes, until slightly softened. Add the crushed garlic, bay leaves, thyme and Parmesan rind and cook for 30 seconds more. Add the grated tomatoes and tomato paste and cook for another 3 minutes, or until the tomatoes cook down slightly. Pour in the 1.7 litres of stock, add ½ teaspoon of salt and a generous grind of pepper, and bring to the boil. Lower the heat to medium and cook for 15 minutes, or until the vegetables have completely softened.

5. Transfer 400g of soup, about 50/50 liquid to solids (avoiding the bay leaves and rind), to a blender, blitzing until completely smooth. Stir the blitzed soup back into the saucepan and return to a medium-high heat. Add the pappardelle, the shredded chicken and a good grind of pepper and cook for 15 minutes, until the pasta is al dente. Discard the bay leaves and the Parmesan rind.

6. Divide the soup between four bowls and top with the basil and chilli, a good grind of pepper and a sprinkling of grated Parmesan.

Make it your own:
- Swap out the pappardelle for other pasta shapes! We also like mafalda pasta.
- Leave out the chilli for a kid-friendly version.

Celebration rice with lamb, chicken and garlic yoghurt

Prep time: *15 minutes*
Cook time: *2 hours*
20 minutes
Soaking time: *1 hour +*

This warming spiced rice is a definite show-stopper, the kind of meal you'd make for a special occasion. We toyed over including this recipe in the book, laborious as it is, but, in all honesty, Noor wouldn't have it any other way. Rice, she believes, deserves to be prized and treasured – taking centre stage at many a family table – and so, make this one as a weekend project, a feast of feasts, a real cause for celebration. Yes, it takes time, but here's a promise that it is oh-so-worth-it.

Serves 8

CHICKEN

1 whole chicken (*1.4kg*)

2 cinnamon sticks

1 onion, *cut into 6 wedges (150g)*

1 head of garlic, *skin on and halved widthways*

1 tsp ground cumin

1 tsp ground cinnamon

2 tbsp olive oil

1½ tbsp lemon juice

5g parsley, *roughly chopped*

salt and black pepper

RICE

2 tbsp olive oil

40g unsalted butter

1 onion, *finely chopped (150g)*

300g minced lamb

3 garlic cloves, *finely chopped*

1½ tsp ground cinnamon

1 tsp ground allspice

400g basmati rice, *washed, soaked in cold water for at least 1 hour and then drained*

1. Put the chicken into a large saucepan, for which you have a lid, along with the cinnamon sticks, onion, garlic, 2 litres of water and 2 teaspoons of salt. Bring to the boil, then lower the heat to medium-low and simmer, covered, for 70 minutes, or until cooked through. Lift out the chicken and, when cool enough, tear into large bite-size chunks, discarding the skin and bones. Place the chicken in a bowl with the ground cumin and cinnamon and set aside. Strain the stock through a sieve set over a large bowl, discarding the solids. Measure out 850ml and keep warm (save the remainder for another use).

2. For the rice, put the oil and half the butter into a large saucepan, for which you have a lid, and place on a medium-high heat. Add the onion and cook for 7 minutes, stirring often, until lightly golden. Add the lamb, garlic and spices and cook for 2 minutes more, stirring often, until the lamb is no longer pink. Add the rice, 700ml of the warm stock, 1¾ teaspoons of salt and a good grind of pepper. Bring to the boil, then reduce the heat to low, cover with the lid and cook for 15 minutes. Take off the heat and allow to sit, covered, for 15 minutes more. Add the remaining butter and set aside.

3. Meanwhile, make the yoghurt sauce by whisking together the yoghurt, garlic, ¾ teaspoon of salt and the remaining 150ml of warm stock in a medium bowl.

4. Put 2 tablespoons of oil into a large sauté pan on a medium-high heat. Add the chicken pieces and cook for 5 minutes, to warm through. Remove from the heat, stir in the lemon juice and parsley and set aside.

> *Get ahead:*
>
> – Cook the chicken the day before, refrigerating the flavourful stock and shredded chicken separately.

GARLIC YOGHURT

500g Greek yoghurt

2 garlic cloves, *crushed*

GARNISH

50g unsalted butter

30g blanched almonds

30g pine nuts

¾ tsp Aleppo chilli, *or ½ tsp regular chilli flakes*

5g picked parsley leaves

4 tbsp pomegranate seeds

5. Make the garnish by putting the butter into a small frying pan on a medium-high heat. Add the almonds and cook for 3 minutes, stirring, until lightly coloured. Add the pine nuts and cook for another 2 minutes, until golden. Remove from the heat and add the Aleppo chilli.

6. Spread the rice over a large, round serving platter. Top with the chicken, then pour over half the garlic yoghurt. Finish with the nuts and butter, followed by the picked parsley and pomegranate seeds. Serve the remaining yoghurt alongside.

Make it your own:

– Swap out the lamb for beef mince, or a mixture of the two, if you wish. The cinnamon rice is a treat on its own, so skip out on everything else if you want to, and eat this with some veggies and a spoonful of yoghurt.

_____

_____

Smoky, creamy pasta with burnt aubergine and tahini

Prep time: *15 minutes*
Cook time: *1 hour 10 minutes*

Burnt aubergines, charred vegetables and nutty tahini are what give this dish a real depth and smokiness, resulting in creamy, vegan pasta made without cream, cheese, butter or any of the usual suspects. If you don't have a griddle pan, char the vegetables in the oven instead.

Serves 4

5 aubergines *(1.25kg), 2 cut into roughly 3–4cm cubes and 3 left whole*

165ml olive oil

1 onion, *cut into 6 wedges (150g)*

2 small vine tomatoes, *left whole (200g)*

1 red chilli *(10g), left whole*

3 tbsp tomato paste

1 tsp paprika

7 garlic cloves, *crushed*

80g tahini

1 tbsp lemon juice

300g dried pasta shells *(conchiglie rigate)*

10g parsley, *roughly chopped*

salt and black pepper

Get ahead:

– Make the burnt aubergine base up to 3 days ahead, reheating it with the pasta water on the day you want to serve it.
– Double or triple the tahini sauce and keep a jar of it in your fridge. Thin it out with a splash of water if needed. Drizzle it over basically everything.

1. Preheat the oven to 220°C fan. Put the aubergine cubes on a large, parchment-lined baking tray and toss with 3 tablespoons of oil, ½ teaspoon of salt and a good grind of pepper. Roast for 30 minutes, stirring halfway through, until deeply browned and softened.

2. Grill your vegetables. Prick the whole aubergines all over with a fork and ventilate your kitchen well. Place a well-greased griddle pan on a high heat and, once smoking, add the aubergines and cook, turning as necessary, for 35 minutes, or until well charred all over. Set aside to cool slightly. Toss the onion, tomatoes and chilli together in a bowl with a tablespoon of oil and grill in the same pan for 10 minutes, turning as necessary, until very well charred and softened. Transfer to a bowl, discarding the chilli stem. Once cool enough to handle, peel and discard the skin and stems of the charred aubergines (it's okay if there is still some skin attached) and add the flesh to the bowl of charred vegetables. You should have roughly 320g of aubergine flesh.

3. Meanwhile, put the tomato paste, paprika, three-quarters of the garlic and 4 tablespoons of oil into a small saucepan on a medium heat and cook, stirring occasionally, until the garlic is fragrant and the tomato paste has turned dark red, about 5 minutes. Transfer this and the grilled vegetables to a food processor, along with ¾ teaspoon of salt and a good grind of pepper, and blitz until completely smooth. Transfer to a large sauté pan and set aside. This is your sauce base.

4. In a small bowl, whisk together the tahini, the remaining garlic, the lemon juice, 70ml of water and a pinch of salt until smooth.

5. Cook the pasta in plenty of salted boiling water for 8 minutes, or until al dente. Reserve 275ml of the pasta water, then drain the pasta well.

6. Add the reserved pasta water and half the roasted aubergine to the sauce base and heat through on a medium-high heat. Add the drained pasta and stir to warm through, about 2 minutes.

7. Toss the remaining roasted aubergine with the parsley and the last 3 tablespoons of oil.

8. Transfer the pasta to a large serving platter with a lip, drizzle over a good amount of the tahini sauce, then spoon over the aubergine and parsley mixture. Serve the extra tahini sauce alongside.

Make it your own:

- Try the aubergine sauce mixed with bulgur wheat, couscous or rice.
- Repurpose the aubergine sauce: thin it out with water to have as a soup with tahini and toasted croutons, or leave out the water entirely, to have as a dip with flatbreads.

_____

_____

Fish koftas in ancho chilli and tomato sauce

Prep time: *30 minutes*
Cook time: *1 hour 10 minutes*

The secret to these koftas is in the sauce: smoky ancho chilli, caraway and cumin adding depth to the whole experience. Tame the spicy kick here by serving with fluffy white rice and some cooling yoghurt.

Serves 4

KOFTAS

500g firm sustainable white fish *(such as cod), boneless and skinless*

4 spring onions, *finely sliced (60g)*

10g dill, *roughly chopped, plus extra picked leaves to serve*

1 green chilli, *deseeded and finely chopped*

1½ tsp finely grated lemon zest

1 egg, *beaten*

30g panko breadcrumbs

3 tbsp olive oil

TOMATO SAUCE

15g dried ancho chillies *(about 1½ chillies), stems removed*

2 tsp caraway seeds, *toasted and roughly crushed*

1 tbsp cumin seeds, *toasted and roughly crushed*

6 garlic cloves, *peeled*

1 onion, *roughly chopped (150g)*

60ml olive oil

1 green chilli, *halved lengthways*

1 tbsp tomato paste

3–4 plum tomatoes *(400g), roughly grated (p. 88) and skins discarded (300g)*

300ml chicken or vegetable stock

2 tsp caster sugar

25g fresh coriander, *roughly chopped*

salt and black pepper

1. First, make the sauce. Put the ancho chillies into a small bowl and cover with plenty of boiling water. Leave to soften for 20 minutes, then drain, discarding the liquid. Roughly chop the chillies, then put them into a food processor along with two-thirds of the caraway and cumin, all the garlic, the onion and 2 tablespoons of oil, and blitz to a coarse paste.

2. Heat the remaining 2 tablespoons of oil in a large sauté pan on a medium-high heat. Add the ancho paste, green chilli and tomato paste and cook for 7 minutes, stirring often, until softened and fragrant. Add the grated tomatoes, stock, 200ml of water, the sugar, half the coriander, 1¼ teaspoons of salt and a good grind of pepper and bring to the boil. Lower the heat to medium and simmer for 15 minutes. Keep warm on a low heat until needed.

3. Meanwhile, make the koftas. Finely chop the fish into ½–1cm pieces. Put them into a large bowl along with the spring onions, dill, chilli, lemon zest, egg, panko breadcrumbs, the remaining coriander, the remaining caraway and cumin, 1 teaspoon of salt and a good grind of pepper and mix well to combine. Form into 12 round fish cakes, roughly 6–7cm in diameter and about 55g in weight. Make sure to press and compact them well, so they stay together when frying.

4. Heat 1½ tablespoons of oil in a large frying pan on a medium-high heat. Add half the koftas and fry for 2½ minutes per side, until golden. Transfer to a plate, then repeat with the remaining oil and koftas.

5. Bring the sauce to a simmer on a medium-high heat. Add the koftas, then turn the heat to medium-low and cook for 10 minutes, to cook through. Leave to sit for about 5 minutes, then top with the extra dill leaves and serve directly from the pan.

Get ahead:

- Make the sauce up to 2 days in advance – it will only intensify as it sits.
- Prepare the kofta mix the day ahead, shaping and pan-frying the day you intend to cook them.

Smoky marinated feta

Prep time: *10 minutes*
Cook time: *15 minutes*

Yotam admits to keeping a jar of this feta in his fridge lately, coming back to it for breakfast (on toast with sliced avocado), supper (over baked potato with egg and chopped salad) or a sneaky pre-bed snack (with a glass of wine . . . or three). Can we blame him? Not really.

Serves 4–6, as a snack

10 garlic cloves, *peeled*

1–2 lemons: *finely shave the skin to get 8 strips and then juice to get ½ tbsp*

4 bay leaves

2½ tsp chipotle chilli flakes

1½ tsp paprika

250ml olive oil

1 tsp flaked sea salt

270g Greek feta *(about 1½ blocks), cut into 2cm cubes*

1. Place a small sauté pan on a medium-high heat. Once very hot, add the garlic and cook for about 3–4 minutes, turning halfway through, until charred on the outside. Add the lemon strips and bay leaves and cook for 90 seconds more, then add the chipotle chilli flakes and cook, stirring continuously, until well toasted and fragrant, about 20 seconds. Remove from the heat and add the paprika, oil and salt, stirring to combine. Leave to cool completely.

2. Stir through the feta, then transfer to a bowl or glass jar with a lid and leave to marinate, at room temperature if eating in the next couple hours or refrigerated (covered) if having it later.

3. If refrigerating, take the feta out of the fridge about an hour or so before you want to serve it, for the oil to come back up to room temperature. Add the lemon juice just before serving.

Get ahead:
– This will keep in the fridge for up to a week in a sealed container. Bring it back up to room temp before spooning it over your favourite things.

Make it your own:
– Add other spices or swap out the chipotle for other types of crushed dried chilli.
– Use the chilli oil instead of cheese for sprinkling over beans, or to spoon over eggs and/or veggies.

Mediterranean-style fried rice with anchovy lemon dressing

Prep time: *20 minutes*
Cook time: *25 minutes*

This Mediterranean take on fried rice has all the crispy and salty bits as well as the very best bit: the crispy 'tahdig' layer at the bottom of the pan. 'Tahdig' is the Persian word referring to the bottom of the pot, where the rice forms a crunchy golden layer of crispy decadence. Also called 'socarrat' in Spain, this scorched rice is the part we look forward to the most.

Serves 2

60ml olive oil

1 green pepper, *stem and seeds discarded and flesh cut roughly into 3cm cubes (150g)*

6 small garlic cloves, *peeled*

1 mild red chilli, *halved lengthways*

4 spring onions, *white and green parts separated, each cut into 3cm lengths (50g)*

5g thyme leaves, *with their soft sprigs*

350g cooked basmati rice

2 eggs

ANCHOVY DRESSING

15g anchovies in oil *(about 5), drained and finely chopped*

2 garlic cloves, *crushed*

½ tsp cumin seeds, *roughly crushed with a pestle and mortar*

2 tbsp olive oil

1 lemon: *finely shave the skin to get 6 strips and then juice to get 1½ tbsp*

1 tbsp roughly chopped parsley leaves

salt and black pepper

1. Make the anchovy dressing by putting the anchovies, garlic, cumin, oil and a good grind of pepper into a small saucepan on a medium heat. As soon as the mixture starts to bubble, remove it from the heat and add the lemon juice. Set aside to cool, then stir in the parsley.

2. Put 1 tablespoon of oil into a large frying pan, for which you have a lid, on a medium-high heat. Add the green pepper pieces and cook for 3 minutes, stirring occasionally, until nicely coloured and softened. Add 2 more tablespoons of oil, the garlic, red chilli and the white parts of the spring onions and cook for 90 seconds more, until they've also taken on some colour. Now add the green parts of the spring onions, the thyme and lemon skin and cook for another 30 seconds, then add the rice, ¼ teaspoon of salt and a good grind of pepper. Stir frequently, breaking apart any clumps with a spoon, and cook for 3 minutes to take on a little colour.

3. Use a spoon to create two wells in the rice mixture, exposing the bottom of the pan. Add 1½ teaspoons of oil to each well, then crack an egg into both and turn the heat down to medium. Sprinkle lightly with salt and pepper, cover with the lid and cook for about 4–5 minutes, or until the whites are set, the yolks are still runny and the bottom of the rice is nice and crispy. Drizzle all over with the anchovy dressing and serve right away.

> *Make it your own:*
> – Lose the fish: replace the anchovies with salty, briny capers.
> – Use up whatever leftover rice you have, jasmine rice or brown, or even a mixture of both!
> – Try it with orzo or giant couscous instead of the rice.

Tomato and courgette loaf with spiced tomato chutney

Prep time: *35 minutes*
Cook time: *2 hours 30 minutes*

Not quite veggie loaf and not quite bread, this savoury loaf is perfect to serve at any and every mealtime. The chutney really is quite special and is what sets this loaf apart, so feel free to double the recipe and use it for other purposes – to eat with cheese and crackers, or to spread on a juicy burger.

Serves 4–6

2 courgettes *(350g), roughly grated*

275g plain flour

2 tsp baking powder

½ tsp bicarbonate of soda

1½ tsp garam masala

1 tsp caster sugar

2 large eggs

75ml olive oil

70g Greek-style yoghurt

150g mature cheddar, *roughly grated*

25g fresh coriander, *roughly chopped*

75g mixed (red and yellow) cherry tomatoes, *halved*

TOMATO CHUTNEY

75ml olive oil

6 garlic cloves, *crushed*

45g fresh ginger, *peeled and finely grated*

2 red chillies, *finely chopped, seeds and all (30g)*

1½ tbsp tomato paste

½ tsp ground turmeric

2 tsp garam masala

1½ tbsp caster sugar

750g tomatoes, *cored and finely chopped, seeds and all*

salt and black pepper

1. Preheat the oven to 180°C fan. Line a standard 900g loaf tin with a piece of baking parchment large enough to cover the bottom and sides.

2. Make the chutney by putting 4 tablespoons of the oil into a large sauté pan on a medium-high heat. Once the oil is hot, add the garlic, ginger and chillies and cook for 2 minutes, stirring occasionally, until fragrant. Add the tomato paste, spices and sugar and cook for a minute more, then add the chopped tomatoes, 1 teaspoon of salt and a good grind of pepper. Bring to a simmer, then turn the heat down to medium and cook for 45 minutes, stirring often, until the tomatoes have completely broken down and the mixture is nice and thick. Measure out 150g of the chutney and set aside to cool.

3. Meanwhile, put the courgettes and ½ teaspoon of salt into a bowl and mix to combine. Set aside for 20 minutes, then transfer the mixture to a clean tea towel and wring out as much liquid as possible. You want about 180g of strained courgette.

4. Put the flour, baking powder, bicarbonate of soda, garam masala, sugar and 1 teaspoon of salt into a large bowl and mix to combine. In a separate bowl, whisk together the eggs, 4 tablespoons of oil and yoghurt, then stir in the cheddar and coriander. Add this, the courgette and the measured 150g of tomato chutney to the flour bowl and mix gently to combine. Transfer the mixture to your lined loaf tin, smoothing out the top to evenly distribute.

5. Arrange the halved cherry tomatoes on top, cut side up, gently pushing them into the surface. Drizzle with another tablespoon of oil and bake for 40 minutes. Remove from the oven and lower the temperature to 170°C fan. Cover with foil, then return to the oven and bake for 45 minutes more, or until a skewer inserted into the centre comes out clean. Set aside to cool in the tin for at least 30 minutes, or longer if time allows.

6. Slice the loaf as you need. Stir the remaining tablespoon of oil into the chutney and serve in a bowl alongside, to spread. If not serving the same day, store well wrapped – it will keep for up to 2 days.

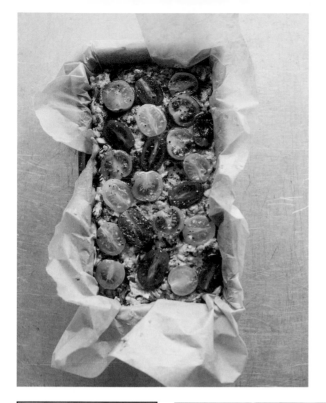

Make it your own:
- Use up other spices in the chutney, such as cumin and coriander or cinnamon and allspice.
- Use other oozy cheeses, such as Gruyère.

_____

_____

_____

Get ahead:
- Make the chutney well in advance and keep in a sealed jar in the fridge for up to a week.

Rice koofteh in spiced tomato sauce

Prep time: *30 minutes*
Cook time: *1 hour 30 minutes*

This is meatballs in tomato sauce, but with a very Persian twist. Yellow split peas are also often thrown into the mix, but we used a bit of gram flour instead. The sauce thickens as it sits, so add a splash more water if you're getting ahead. Eat these koofteh with some veggies and a spoonful of yoghurt, if you like.

Serves 6

250g basmati rice, *washed until the water runs clear and drained well*

500g beef or lamb mince *(15% fat), or a mixture of both*

½ onion, *roughly grated on a box grater (60g)*

40g parsley, *finely chopped, plus extra picked leaves to serve*

40g fresh coriander, *finely chopped*

40g dill, *finely chopped, plus extra picked leaves to serve*

1 large egg

30g gram flour, *or rice flour*

½ tsp chilli flakes

1½ tsp ground cumin

1½ tsp ground cinnamon

½ tsp ground turmeric

salt and black pepper

TOMATO SAUCE

3 tbsp olive oil, *plus extra for shaping the koofteh*

1 large onion, *finely chopped*

6 garlic cloves, *crushed*

350g tomatoes *(about 3), finely chopped*

70g tomato paste

60g soft dried apricots, *quartered (or 1½ teaspoons caster sugar)*

10 cardamom pods, *roughly bashed open with a pestle and mortar*

½ tsp chilli flakes

1½ tsp ground cumin

1½ tsp ground coriander

1 tsp ground turmeric

1. Cook the rice for 10 minutes in plenty of boiling salted water, until just cooked through. Drain well in a sieve and set aside to cool (you should be left with about 630g of cooked rice).

2. Make the koofteh by putting the beef or lamb mince, onion, herbs, egg, gram flour and spices into a large bowl with 1¼ teaspoons of salt and a good grind of pepper. Add the cooled rice and use your hands to knead the mixture for about 5–6 minutes, until the rice grains are well crushed and the mixture is quite paste-like. This is a great arm workout, so switch arms halfway through.

3. Using well-oiled hands, shape the mixture into 12 large balls, roughly 120g in weight. Refrigerate until ready to use.

4. Make the sauce by putting the oil into a large, wide-based sauté pan, for which you have a lid, on a medium-high heat. Add the onion and cook for 7 minutes, stirring occasionally, until golden. Add the garlic and cook for 30 seconds more, then add the tomatoes, tomato paste, apricots and spices. Cook for 4 minutes, stirring occasionally, until the tomatoes have started to break down. Add 850ml of water, 1¼ teaspoons of salt and a good grind of pepper, and bring to a gentle simmer. Add the koofteh, one at a time, then lower the heat to medium-low, cover with the lid and leave to cook for 45 minutes, until the koofteh are cooked through and the sauce has reduced slightly (it will still be quite brothy, but will thicken as it sits).

5. Top with the extra picked parsley and dill leaves and serve warm, directly from the pan.

Make it your own:

– Use up whatever herbs you have on hand (tarragon and chives would be great here!) and whichever spices.
– Try this using other cooked grains instead, such as brown rice or bulgur wheat.

_____

_____

_____

Herby cabbage and potato gratin with Gruyère and ricotta

Prep time: *15 minutes*
Cook time: *2 hours 10 minutes*

Multiple layers of flavour make this gratin subtly special, the first being two types of garlic: sweet, sticky and roasted, and then raw and pungent. The second being a multitude of herbs and cheeses in between layers of potato, shallots and cabbage. It is as lovely to look at as it is to eat, and can be served as is, or alongside your protein of choice.

Serves 4

2 heads of garlic, *skin on and top fifth cut off to expose the cloves, plus 3 extra peeled cloves*

65ml olive oil

450g Désirée potatoes *(about 4), skin on and sliced 3mm thick*

3 banana shallots, *finely sliced on a mandolin or by hand (130g)*

2½ tsp smoked paprika

1 pointed sweet cabbage, *base trimmed, thick stalks removed and leaves separated (400g)*

20g basil, *finely chopped*

10g tarragon, *finely chopped*

20g parsley, *finely chopped*

3–4 spring onions, *finely sliced (50g)*

2 lemons: *finely grate the zest to get 1½ tbsp and then juice to get 1 tbsp*

200g whole-milk ricotta

150g Gruyère, *roughly grated*

250ml chicken or vegetable stock

salt and black pepper

1. Preheat the oven to 200°C fan.

2. Drizzle the garlic heads with 1 teaspoon of oil and sprinkle with a pinch of salt and pepper. Wrap each individually in foil and roast for 40 minutes, until softened and golden. Remove the foil and, when cool enough to handle, squeeze out the cloves, discarding the papery skins.

3. Meanwhile, prepare the rest of the vegetables. Combine the potatoes, shallots and paprika in a bowl with 2 tablespoons of oil, ¾ teaspoon of salt and plenty of pepper.

4. Toss the cabbage leaves together with 1 tablespoon of oil, ⅓ teaspoon of salt and plenty of pepper.

5. Finely chop the three extra garlic cloves and mix together with all the herbs, the spring onions, lemon zest and the roasted garlic. Reserve a quarter of this mixture and set aside, to serve.

6. Assemble the bake. Arrange a third of the cabbage leaves in the bottom of a 26cm x 34cm high-sided baking dish. Cover with half the potato mixture and a third of the herb mixture. Dot half of the ricotta and Gruyère randomly over the herbs. Repeat this once more, then top with a final layer of cabbage and the remaining third of the herb mixture.

7. Combine the stock, lemon juice and ¼ teaspoon of salt and pour this evenly over the bake, lifting some of the cabbage leaves up so the liquid sinks down. Cover tightly with foil and bake for 80 minutes, until the vegetables are soft. Drizzle over the remaining tablespoon of oil and return to the oven, uncovered, for 15 minutes, to brown. Leave to cool for 10 minutes, then top with the reserved herb mixture.

Make it your own:
– Play with your cheeses!
– Play with your spices!

_____

_____

_____

_____

_____

Make it your own:

- Swap out the butternut squash for sweet potato or pumpkin.
- Alternatively, serve the butternut mash with flatbread instead of the pomlettes.
- Eat these pomlettes alongside the smooshed carrots (p. 68).

_____

_____

Spiced butternut mash with pancake omelettes (pomlettes)

Prep time: *25 minutes*
Cook time: *1 hour 10 minutes*

When we get asked what inspires us, our responses usually vary: home, friends, things we grew up eating, places we've visited, etc. Oftentimes, though, what inspires us at the OTK is each other – adding our own identities to something both new and familiar. These pancakes-omelettes are the brainchild of Claudine, who struggled to find flour during lockdown and resourcefully used up the arrowroot in her cupboard, keeping these wonderfully gluten-free. Noor quickly renamed the pancake-omelettes 'pomlettes', and found they were the perfect vehicle for this spiced butternut mash. Breakfast sorted.

Serves 4, generously

SPICED BUTTERNUT

600g butternut squash, *peeled, deseeded and cut into roughly 4cm chunks*

105ml olive oil

1 red onion, *halved and thinly sliced (120g)*

6 garlic cloves, *crushed*

40g fresh ginger, *peeled and finely grated*

2 green chillies, *finely chopped, seeds and all*

2 tsp garam masala

1 vine tomato, *finely chopped (100g)*

1 tsp cumin seeds

20 fresh curry leaves *(from 2 sprigs)*

1 tsp black mustard seeds

salt

120g Greek-style yoghurt, *to serve*

1 lime, *cut into 4 wedges to serve*

PANCAKES

9 eggs

90g arrowroot flour

90g Greek-style yoghurt

150ml whole milk

½ tsp ground turmeric

60ml olive oil

1. Preheat the oven to 220°C fan.

2. Put the butternut squash, 1½ tablespoons of oil, 120ml of water and ½ teaspoon of salt into a 30cm x 20cm baking dish. Roast for 45 minutes, stirring halfway through, until nicely browned and the liquid has evaporated.

3. Meanwhile, put 2½ tablespoons of oil into a large sauté pan on a medium-high heat. Once hot, cook the onion for 8–10 minutes, stirring occasionally, until softened and browned. Add the garlic, ginger and chillies and cook for 3 minutes more, stirring often. Add the garam masala, tomato and 3 tablespoons of water and cook for 4 minutes, until the tomato has broken down. Off the heat, add the roasted butternut squash and ½ teaspoon of salt and use a fork to roughly mash everything together. Keep warm until ready to serve.

4. Make the tempered oil by heating the remaining 3 tablespoons of oil in a small frying pan on a medium-high heat. Add the cumin seeds and curry leaves and cook for 60–90 seconds, or until the leaves turn translucent.

Remove from the heat and add the mustard seeds.

5. Make the pancake mixture by putting everything except the oil into a food processor, along with 1 teaspoon of salt, and blitzing until smooth.

6. Heat 1 teaspoon of oil in a medium non-stick frying pan over a medium-high heat. Ladle about 65g of the pancake batter into the pan, swirling to spread it around the base, and cook for 30 seconds on each side, or until nicely browned. Transfer to a plate and keep warm under a tea towel. Repeat with the remaining batter and oil to make 12 pancakes in total. Speed this up by using two frying pans.

7. When ready to serve, stir half the tempered oil into the butternut squash mixture and transfer to a bowl, spooning the remaining oil and solids on top. Arrange the pancakes on a large platter (they don't need to be neat). Put the yoghurt into a bowl and nestle this and the butternut squash bowl around the pancakes with the lime wedges. Get everyone involved in building their own pancakes.

Beyond potato salad

Prep time: *25 minutes*
Cook time: *50 minutes*

This is a spin on the – very retro – salad Olivieh, a mayonnaise-based potato salad with many different variations, depending on whose household you're in. Some add shredded chicken, peas or mashed carrots, some eliminate the egg. We kept this version veggie, using lots of lemon, herbs and toasted seeds to jazz it up. It's a real 'use-up-what-you-have' type of dish, suitable to take to picnics or to serve as a barbecue side.

Serves 6, as a side

650g King Edward potatoes, *scrubbed clean, or another floury potato such as Maris Piper*

5 large eggs

80g mayonnaise

220g Greek-style yoghurt

3½ tbsp lemon juice

105ml olive oil

30g gherkins, *thinly sliced into rounds*

10g tarragon leaves, *roughly torn*

10g chives, *sliced into 1cm lengths*

1½ tsp coriander seeds, *roughly crushed with a pestle and mortar and toasted*

¾ tsp nigella seeds, *toasted*

¾ tsp sesame seeds, *toasted*

½ tsp Aleppo chilli, *or ¼ tsp regular chilli flakes*

salt and black pepper

1. Put the potatoes into a medium saucepan, for which you have a lid, and pour over enough water to cover by about 4cm. Season with 2 teaspoons of salt and bring to a simmer on a medium-high heat. Turn the heat to medium, cover with the lid and cook for 25 minutes, or until the potatoes are easily pierced with a fork. Drain and, when cool enough to handle, peel and discard the skins and roughly mash the potatoes in a large bowl to give you a lumpy mash.

2. Meanwhile, cook the eggs in boiling water for 8 minutes, or until just hard-boiled. Drain, peel and discard the shells, then use a box grater to roughly grate the eggs, adding them to the potato bowl.

3. In a medium bowl, whisk together the mayonnaise, yoghurt, 2½ tablespoons of lemon juice, 2 tablespoons of oil, 1 teaspoon of salt and a generous grind of pepper. Add this to the potato mixture and mix well to combine. Transfer to a large serving plate, spreading to create a slight well in the centre. Cover and refrigerate if not serving right away.

4. Mix together the gherkins, herbs, the remaining tablespoon of lemon juice and 5 tablespoons of oil, ⅛ teaspoon of salt and a good grind of pepper. Spoon this all over the potato mixture.

5. Mix together all the toasted seeds and the chilli and sprinkle this all over the top. Serve at room temperature or cold.

Get ahead:
– Make the day before and keep refrigerated, loosening it with a splash of water to serve, if needed.

Any grilled veg with mustard and Parmesan dressing

Prep time: *25 minutes*
Cook time: *1 hour*

Big plates of grilled vegetables never really go out of fashion. The key is to treat each vegetable individually, giving it the unique love and attention it deserves to make sure it shows up to the table looking its absolute best. We dress our grilled veggies in this sharp and cheesy dressing, but they do like a versatile wardrobe – so feel free to experiment with different vinaigrettes and sauces.

Serves 4

1 cooked baking potato *(250g), skin on and cut into 1cm slices*

400g bunch of thick-stemmed asparagus, *woody ends trimmed (250g)*

2 red peppers, *stems and seeds discarded and each pepper quartered (300g)*

2 red onions, *each cut into 4 x 1½cm-thick rounds (240g)*

60ml olive oil, *plus extra for greasing*

6 small garlic cloves, *peeled*

2 baby gem lettuces, *core removed and leaves separated (150g)*

5g picked parsley leaves, *with some stem attached*

½ tsp fennel seeds, *toasted and roughly crushed with a pestle and mortar*

salt and black pepper

MUSTARD PARMESAN DRESSING

¾ tbsp Dijon mustard

2 garlic cloves, *crushed*

25g Parmesan, *finely grated*

3 tbsp lemon juice

75ml olive oil

1. Put the potato, asparagus, peppers and onions into four separate bowls, and toss each with a tablespoon of oil and a pinch each of salt and pepper.

2. Make the dressing by putting all the ingredients into a bowl with ¼ teaspoon of salt and a good grind of pepper and whisking until combined.

3. Place a well-greased griddle pan on a high heat until smoking. Grill each of the vegetables separately, until nicely charred and softened. Grill the peppers for about 15–20 minutes, the onions for 4 minutes on each side, the potatoes for 2 minutes on each side, the asparagus for 7 minutes in total and, lastly, the garlic cloves for a minute on each side. Set aside each of the grilled vegetables separately and, while they're still warm, spoon over some of the dressing to nicely coat them.

4. Toss the gem lettuce and parsley leaves together in any remaining dressing and transfer to a large plate. Arrange the grilled vegetables on the same plate and sprinkle with the fennel seeds to serve.

Make it your own:
– Play around with whatever vegetables you have on hand. Pre-cook those that need longer cooking, such as root vegetables.

_____

_____

_____

Cream of tomato soup with buttery onions and orecchiette

Prep time: *15 minutes*
Cook time: *1 hour 10 minutes*

This is basically Heinz tomato soup but amplified, thanks to the added oomph of habanero chilli and sweet buttery onions. This makes the soup a little more grown-up, so leave out the chilli if you're making this kid-friendly or if you're not that into heat.

Serves 4

60g unsalted butter

90ml olive oil

3 onions, *finely chopped* (540g)

2 large garlic cloves, *crushed*

400g sweet red cherry or datterini tomatoes

4 tbsp tomato paste

10g basil leaves, *roughly torn*

1 dried habanero chilli (optional)

500ml vegetable or chicken stock (or water)

200g dried orecchiette pasta

2 tbsp double cream (or more, if you like)

salt and black pepper

1. Put the butter, 3 tablespoons of oil, the onions and 1 teaspoon of salt into a large sauté pan on a medium heat and cook for 18–20 minutes, stirring often, until soft and deeply golden brown. Lower the heat if they get too brown.

2. Transfer two-thirds of the fried onions to a bowl and stir in the remaining 3 tablespoons of oil.

3. Return the pan with the remaining onions to a medium heat, add the garlic and fry for 2 minutes. Add the tomatoes, tomato paste, basil, habanero (if using) and 2 teaspoons of salt and fry for 7 minutes, stirring often. Increase the heat to medium-high, add the stock, 300ml of water and a good grind of pepper and bring to a simmer. Lower the heat to medium and cook for 12 minutes. Remove the habanero (if using) and squeeze to discard any liquid. Finely chop the habanero and stir into the bowl with the reserved fried onions.

4. Leave the soup to cool for 5–10 minutes, so it's not dangerously hot, then transfer to a blender and blitz until completely smooth.

5. Meanwhile, cook the orecchiette until al dente, then drain and divide between four bowls. Pour over the soup, then spoon over the cream and the onion mixture.

Make it your own:
- Leave out the habanero or swap out for another milder chilli such as ancho or chipotle.
- Veganise it: leave out the cream and use extra olive oil instead of butter for the onions.
- Swap out the orecchiette for different pasta shapes or some cooked rice.

_____

_____

Gnocchi with sumac onions and brown butter pine nuts

Prep time: *25 minutes*
Cook time: *1 hour 35 minutes*

We use sumac onions liberally at the Test Kitchen, mostly because they lend just the right amount of acidity and sweetness (when cooked) or sharpness (when raw). The Middle East meets Italy here, and we can all vouch that sumac and gnocchi get along splendidly. If you don't have time to make gnocchi, then you can always use store-bought. Our very own Gitai says that he often uses jarred butter beans in place of the gnocchi as an even healthier option.

Serves 4, as a starter or light lunch

1.4kg Maris Piper potatoes, *skin on and scrubbed clean, then pricked all over with a fork*

3 egg yolks, *lightly beaten*

110g plain flour, *sifted*

2 tbsp olive oil, *plus extra for drizzling*

70g unsalted butter

35g pine nuts

2 tbsp lemon juice

5g parsley leaves, *roughly chopped*

salt and black pepper

80g crème fraîche, *to serve (optional)*

SUMAC ONIONS

2 tbsp olive oil

3 red onions, *halved and thinly sliced (360g)*

½ tsp salt

4 garlic cloves, *crushed*

4 tsp sumac

Get ahead:

– Make and boil the gnocchi a day in advance. Spread out on a well-oiled tray and refrigerate until needed.

---

1. Preheat the oven to 220°C fan. Place the potatoes directly on the middle rack of your oven and bake for 45 minutes, or until cooked through.

2. Meanwhile, make the onions. Heat the oil in a large sauté pan on a medium-high heat. Add the onions and ½ teaspoon of salt and cook for 12–15 minutes, stirring occasionally, until softened and browned. Add the garlic and cook for 2 minutes more, until fragrant. Stir through the sumac and remove from the heat. Transfer the mixture to a bowl and rinse out the pan.

3. While still hot (use a tea towel or gloves), slice open the potatoes and scoop out their insides, discarding the skins: you want about 600g. Use a potato ricer to finely mash the potato directly on to a clean work surface. Lightly spread the potato out so it's not all in one pile and sprinkle evenly with the egg yolks, followed by the flour and ½ teaspoon of salt. Use a pastry cutter or bench scraper to cut into the mixture, chopping repeatedly to evenly distribute everything. Use your fingers to gather everything together into a ball (don't knead the mixture at all). Transfer the mixture to a piping bag and set it aside.

4. Bring a large saucepan of well-salted water to the boil on a medium-high heat. Snip off the end of your piping bag to create an opening about 2cm wide. Pipe 3cm lengths of the gnocchi into the water (about 12 at a time), using a small sharp knife to release the dough, and cook for 1–2 minutes, or until the gnocchi float to the surface. Use a slotted spoon to transfer the gnocchi to a parchment-lined tray, drizzling with a little oil to prevent them from sticking. Continue this way until you've cooked all the gnocchi, about 4–5 batches.

5. Add 1 tablespoon of oil to the rinsed-out sauté pan from earlier and place on a medium-high heat. Add a third of the gnocchi and cook for 4 minutes, until golden all over. Transfer to a parchment-lined tray and continue in this way, adding ½ tablespoon of oil and a third of the gnocchi each time.

6. Melt the butter in the same pan on a medium-high heat. Add the pine nuts, ½ teaspoon of salt and a good grind of pepper and cook for 2 minutes, until golden. Turn the heat to low and add back all the gnocchi, sumac onions, lemon juice and parsley, stirring gently to combine. Serve the crème fraîche alongside, if using.

Make it your own:

– Save time and use shop-bought gnocchi, Gitai's butter beans suggestion (see intro) or roasted diced potatoes.

– Double up on the sumac onions and fold them into mashed potatoes or pasta!

_____

_____

The

IS YOUR

Freezer

FRIEND

The freezer is your friend

The freezer is your most loyal friend: the kind of pal that'll take what you don't want, preserve it and then give it back to you when you're good and ready (all the while never losing its cool). We're sometimes guilty of neglecting it, but then it's like digging through a treasure chest, filled to the brim with valuable finds and ice crystals. We have a little theory that much insight can be gained when having a rummage through a person's freezer. In typical 'I'll show you mine if you show me yours' fashion, we had a quick Test Kitchen reveal.

What's in our freezers? Our answers vary . . . greatly. Chaya says Mauritian shrimp paste and fish fingers, her love for seafood very apparent. Yotam says sliced sourdough and pistachio ice cream (the good kind only, he emphasises). Verena says dough, every single dough you can possibly think of, but mostly pie dough, ready to be baked at a moment's craving. Noor says nuts, fresh dates and za'atar – there's no guessing which part of the world she's from. Ixta says Scotch bonnets and tortillas, ready to be turned into a taco when taco inspiration strikes. Gitai says berries and Parmesan rinds, a little bit fruity and a whole lotta funky. And, saving the best for last, Tara says frozen lasagne for the kids, and vodka for the adults (smart choices on both counts).

All in all, we decided that building a chapter on the various freezer identities out there would prove challenging, unique as they are. We therefore stuck to the universal freezer-favourites: frozen veggies like peas in our peas, tahini and za'atar (p. 182); frozen pastry like filo in our curried cauliflower cheese filo pie (p. 179); frozen seafood like the frozen prawns used in our cobb salad (p. 184); and frozen fruits like the mixed berries in our skillet berries, bread and browned butter (p. 204). We know this just covers the bases, but here's hoping these recipes break the ice.

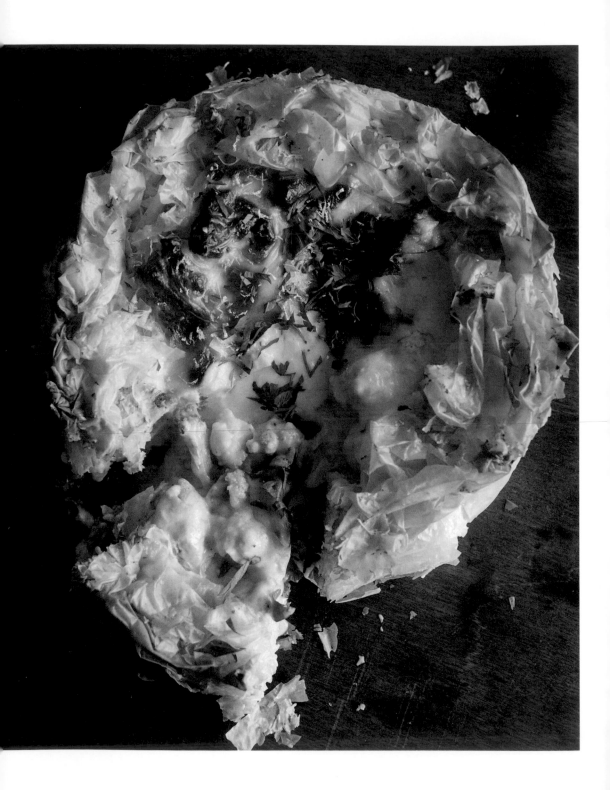

Curried cauliflower cheese filo pie

Prep time: *20 minutes*
Cook time: *1 hour 45 minutes*

Cauliflower cheese, but make it pie. This dish was once described as 'molten-hot-cheese-lava' and we think that's pretty fitting for the ultimate comfort of comfort foods.

Serves 4, generously

1 large cauliflower, *trimmed and cut into bite-size florets (700g)*

2 tsp mild curry powder

3 tbsp olive oil

100g unsalted butter, *50g cut into roughly 3cm cubes and 50g melted*

75g plain flour

675ml whole milk

2 garlic cloves, *crushed*

1½ tbsp English mustard

150g mature cheddar, *roughly grated*

6 sheets of good-quality filo pastry *(we use feuilles de filo)*

salt and black pepper

1 tbsp roughly chopped parsley, *to serve*

1½ tsp lemon zest, *to serve*

1. Preheat the oven to 180°C fan. Line the bottom and sides of a 23cm springform cake tin with baking parchment.

2. Put the cauliflower on a large, parchment-lined baking tray and toss with the curry powder, half the oil, ½ teaspoon of salt and a good grind of pepper. Roast for about 20 minutes, until cooked through and lightly coloured. Set aside, and turn the oven temperature down to 170°C fan.

3. Meanwhile, make the béchamel. Put the cubed butter into a medium saucepan on a medium-high heat and, once melted, whisk in the flour and cook for 1–2 minutes – it should start to smell nutty (like popcorn). Turn the heat down to medium and slowly add the milk a little at a time, whisking continuously to prevent any lumps, until incorporated and the sauce is smooth. Cook, whisking often, for about 7 minutes, until thickened slightly. Off the heat, stir in the garlic, mustard, cheese and ¼ teaspoon of salt until the cheese has melted.

4. Keep your filo sheets under a damp tea towel to prevent them from drying out. In a bowl, combine the melted butter and the remaining 1½ tablespoons of oil and keep to one side.

5. Working one sheet at a time, brush the exposed side of the filo with the butter mixture and drape it into your prepared tin (buttered side up), pushing it down gently to fit. Continue in this way with the next filo sheet, brushing it with butter and then laying it over the bottom sheet, rotating it slightly so the overhang drapes over the sides at a different angle. Do this with all six sheets.

6. Spoon half the béchamel into the base and top with the roasted cauliflower florets. Spoon over the remaining béchamel, then crimp up the overhang so that it creates a messy 'scrunched-up' border around the edges, leaving the centre of the pie exposed.

7. Brush the top of the filo border with the remaining butter mixture, then transfer the tin to a baking tray and bake for 30 minutes.

8. Using a tea towel to help you, carefully release the outer circle of the springform tin and return the pie to the oven for another 20 25 minutes, or until the sides are nicely coloured and everything is golden and bubbling. Leave to settle for 15 minutes.

9. Top the pie with the parsley and lemon zest and serve warm.

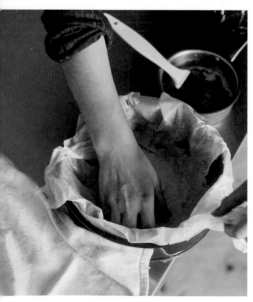

Make it your own:

- Try using shortcrust or puff pastry instead, being mindful of cooking times.
- Play with your cheese! Anything oozy and melty would work.
- Spice it up. Curry powder not enough? Add chilli heat.

_____

_____

Peas, tahini and za'atar

Prep time: *15 minutes*
Cook time: *10 minutes*

There are always bags of frozen peas in our freezers, ready to be tossed into salads or stews or blitzed into this easy pea dip. Serve with your choice of crudité or – our favourite – warm pita breads (p. 23).

Serves 4–6, as part of a mezze spread

500g frozen peas, *defrosted*
65g tahini
40g parsley, *roughly chopped*
20g picked mint leaves
3 tbsp za'atar
2 lemons: *finely grate the zest to get 2 tsp and then juice to get 3 tbsp*
105ml olive oil
40g breakfast radishes (about 4), *thinly sliced on a mandolin or by hand*
2 spring onions, *thinly sliced at an angle (25g)*
salt and black pepper

1. Set aside 50g of peas in a medium bowl for later.

2. Put the remaining peas, the tahini, herbs, 2 tablespoons of za'atar, the lemon zest and juice, 3 tablespoons of oil, 1¼ teaspoons of salt and a good grind of pepper into a food processor and blitz into a smooth paste. Spread out on a large plate, using a spoon to create a shallow well in the centre.

3. To the reserved peas add the radishes, spring onions, 1 tablespoon of oil, ⅛ teaspoon of salt and a good grind of pepper and toss to combine.

4. In a small bowl, whisk together the remaining tablespoon of za'atar and the last 3 tablespoons of oil.

5. Drizzle the za'atar oil all over the pea dip, and top with the radish mixture.

Make it your own:
- Use any equivalent of soft herbs you have on hand (dill and tarragon would be great here).
- Swap out the tahini for Greek-style yoghurt.

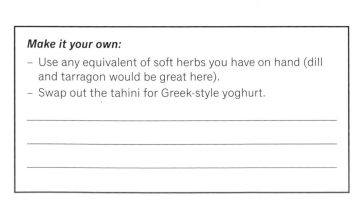

Cobb salad with mango and lime dressing

Prep time: *35 minutes*
Cook time: *40 minutes*

Cobb salads slide easily into the OTK ethos, as they're all about using up what you have to create something playful and vibrant. Here we invite you to the Cobb salad playground, using this recipe as a baseline. Dig through your cupboards, rummage through your fridge and freezer, use what you can and what you have, and then build from there – all the while keeping the spirit of abundance and fun.

Serves 4 as a main

6 slices of prosciutto *(60g)*

2 large eggs

60ml olive oil

350g asparagus, *woody ends trimmed and spears cut widthways into 3 (220g)*

300g frozen sweetcorn kernels, *defrosted*

350g frozen or fresh extra-large peeled prawns, *defrosted if frozen and patted dry*

200g datterini or regular cherry tomatoes, *halved*

1 large iceberg lettuce *(500g), chopped into bite-size pieces*

15g picked fresh coriander leaves, *with some stem attached*

flesh of 1 large avocado, *thinly sliced*

1 small red onion *(80g), very thinly sliced into rounds*

½ lime

salt and black pepper

MANGO LIME DRESSING

200g frozen or fresh mango, *defrosted if frozen*

75ml lime juice

60ml olive oil

2 anchovies in oil, *drained and roughly chopped*

5g fresh coriander, *finely chopped*

1 red chilli, *deseeded and finely chopped (10g)*

1. Preheat the oven to 170°C fan.

2. Lay out the prosciutto on a large, parchment-lined baking tray and bake for 15 minutes, until starting to crisp up. Leave to cool completely.

3. Meanwhile, boil the eggs for 7–8 minutes. Drain, run under cold water, then peel and cut each egg into quarters. Sprinkle lightly with salt and pepper and set aside.

4. Make the dressing. Put the mango, lime juice, oil and anchovies into a food processor or blender and blitz until smooth. Transfer to a bowl and stir in the coriander, chilli, ⅓ teaspoon of salt and a good grind of pepper.

5. Heat 1½ teaspoons of oil in a large sauté pan on a medium-high heat. Add the asparagus, ¼ teaspoon of salt and a good grind of pepper and cook for 4 minutes, to soften and char. Transfer to a tray, then add 1 tablespoon of oil to the same pan along with the sweetcorn, ¼ teaspoon of

salt and a good grind of pepper and cook, stirring occasionally, for 4 minutes, to char in places. Set aside, separately, and add another tablespoon of oil to the pan, turning the heat to high. Once very hot, add half the prawns, ¼ teaspoon of salt and a good grind of pepper and cook for 3 minutes, until just cooked through and browned. Set aside, separately, and continue in the same way with another tablespoon of oil, the remaining prawns and seasoning.

6. Toss the tomatoes together with a pinch of salt and pepper and 1½ teaspoons of oil.

7. In a large bowl, combine the lettuce, coriander, a third of the dressing, ¼ teaspoon of salt and a good grind of pepper. Spread out on a large serving platter. In separate piles, top the lettuce with the tomato, avocado, onion, sweetcorn, asparagus, eggs, prosciutto and prawns. Squeeze over the lime half, and drizzle over another third of the dressing, serving any extra alongside.

> **Get ahead:**
> – Make the dressing up to 2 days in advance.

Make it your own:

- Bring your Cobb salad to life by using up what you have.
- Vegify it: swap out the prawns for tofu or seared mushrooms, replace the anchovies with capers, and leave out the prosciutto.

_____

_____

_____

Braised green beans with tomato, cardamom and garlic

Prep time: *15 minutes*
Cook time: *55 minutes*

Slow-cooking green beans makes them wonderfully soft and comforting, despite not keeping their bright green hue. You can use frozen green beans as we do here, or fresh – depending on what you can find.

Serves 4, as a side

150g datterini or regular cherry tomatoes

550g vine tomatoes *(about 4–5), roughly chopped*

120ml olive oil

1 onion, *halved and finely sliced (180g)*

10 garlic cloves, *thinly sliced*

8 whole cardamom pods, *lightly bashed open with a pestle and mortar*

1½ tsp ground cumin

½ tsp chilli flakes

450g frozen green beans, *defrosted and halved at an angle*

15g fresh coriander, *roughly chopped, plus extra picked leaves to serve*

salt and black pepper

1. Place a large sauté pan, for which you have a lid, on a high heat. Once very hot, cook the datterini/cherry tomatoes for 5 minutes, to char all over. Transfer the tomatoes to a bowl and let the pan cool slightly.

2. Put the vine tomatoes into a food processor and blitz until puréed. Set aside until needed.

3. Return the pan to a medium-high heat with 5 tablespoons of oil. Once the oil is hot, add the onion and cook for about 6 minutes, until softened and lightly browned. Add two-thirds of the garlic and all the cardamom and cook for 2 minutes more, until the garlic has taken on some colour. Add the spices and cook for 30 seconds, then stir through the blitzed tomatoes, 1½ teaspoons of salt and a good grind of pepper and cook for 7 minutes, stirring occasionally, until thickened. Add 250ml of water and cook for 8 minutes more, then reduce the heat to medium, add the green beans, cover with the lid and cook for 12 minutes. Give everything a stir, add the charred tomatoes, then replace the lid and cook for a final 8 minutes, until the beans are very soft. Stir in the chopped coriander.

4. Meanwhile, put the remaining 3 tablespoons of oil and the remaining sliced garlic into a small frying pan and place it on a medium heat. Cook for about 8 minutes, stirring occasionally, until the garlic is golden and crispy.

5. When ready to serve, transfer the green beans to a large shallow bowl or platter. Top with the picked coriander and spoon over the fried garlic and its oil. Serve at room temperature.

> *Get ahead:*
> – Make the whole dish, minus the crispy garlic and fresh coriander, the day before. The flavours will only intensify overnight.

Make it your own:
- Replace the frozen green beans with mangetout or okra.
- Serve this warm, with rice or braised meat.

_____

_____

_____

Vampire-slaying toum

Prep time: *20 minutes*
Cook time: *15 minutes*

Toum, which literally translates to 'garlic' in Arabic, is a Levantine condiment made by whipping together raw garlic and oil with a good amount of lemon juice. It is potent enough to ward off even the most persistent of vampires and is most definitely not for the garlic averse among us. Use it sparingly, and if you find it *too* potent, swirl through some Greek-style yoghurt, as we do in the following two recipes. Make sure to use a neutral-tasting oil here, such as sunflower oil, and not olive oil – it'll ensure the toum stays white and fluffy and won't detract from the intensely pungent garlic flavour. This recipe will most likely make more than you need, but toum is stable enough to have a long shelf life. Once made, store it in a sealed jar in the fridge; it'll keep for up to 4 weeks and goes really well with crispy potatoes, grilled meat (particularly when rich and fatty) and just about anything battered and fried. Lastly, toum loses its intensity the longer it sits, so for the more faint of heart, make this a few days in advance of when you need it.

Makes 350g

100g garlic cloves, *peeled (about 3 heads) – make sure they are well dried*

300ml sunflower oil *(250g by weight), or another neutral-tasting oil*

75ml lemon juice

salt

1. Halve the garlic cloves lengthways and use a small, sharp knife to remove and discard the inner part (some will look green or similar to a white twig).

2. Transfer the cored-out garlic cloves to a food processor along with ¼ teaspoon of salt and 2 tablespoons of the oil. Blitz until very smooth and aerated, about 3 minutes, stopping to scrape down the bowl a couple times. With the machine still running, very slowly drizzle in about 60ml (a fifth) of the oil, followed by a tablespoon of lemon juice. Continue in this way, alternating between oil and lemon juice and ending with the oil. Do this very slowly and steadily; you don't want the toum to split at all. You should be left with a white, fluffy and homogenised mixture. Transfer to a sterilised, sealed jar and store refrigerated; it'll keep for up to 4 weeks.

Buckwheat-battered fish with toum and pickled chillies

Prep time: *25 minutes*
Cook time: *50 minutes*

This gluten-free take on battered fish and mayo is a massive departure from anything traditional, but it works, with the buckwheat adding a lovely, nutty flavour to the batter. Swap the toum out with some store-bought mayonnaise or yoghurt, if you like, although it really does make the dish super special.

Serves 4

1 red chilli, *thinly sliced, seeds and all (10g)*

2 tbsp apple cider vinegar

100g toum *(p. 190)*

100g Greek-style yoghurt

½ tbsp finely chopped chives

1 tbsp olive oil

salt and black pepper

FISH

4 frozen fillets of sustainable white fish, *boneless and skinless, defrosted (560g)*

700ml sunflower oil, *for deep-frying*

55g cornflour

55g rice flour *(not the glutinous kind)*

50g buckwheat flour

2 tbsp black and white sesame seeds, *toasted*

185ml sparkling water

1. Put the chillies, vinegar and a tiny pinch of salt into a small bowl and set aside to pickle while you continue with the rest.

2. Pat dry the fish and season well with ½ teaspoon of salt and a good grind of pepper. Put the sunflower oil into a large, high-sided and non-stick sauté pan on a medium-high heat and, while it's heating up, make the batter.

3. In a large bowl, whisk together the flours, sesame seeds and ¾ teaspoon of salt, then slowly whisk in the sparkling water to make a thick, smooth and pourable batter.

4. Drop a little bit of the batter into the oil to test it's hot enough. It should immediately start to sizzle and take on a little bit of colour. Frying two at a time, dip a piece of fish into the batter until nicely coated and then drop it straight into the hot oil. Fry for 7 minutes, turning over halfway through, until lightly golden and cooked through. Transfer to a tray lined with kitchen paper and continue this way with the rest.

5. In a small bowl, combine the toum and the yoghurt. Top with the chives and olive oil.

6. When ready to serve, place the fish on a large platter and spoon over the pickled chillies. Serve the toum mixture alongside.

Make it your own:
- We love this gluten-free batter so much, and can vouch that it works well with just about anything. If you're not into fish, then thinly sliced vegetables or tofu would work well here too.
- Swap out the rice or buckwheat flour for the equivalent amount of plain flour.

Broad bean and herb salad with toum

Prep time: *25 minutes*
Cook time: *20 minutes*

This fresh, sharp salad and toum-yoghurt makes a lovely side to heartier dishes and fatty meats.

Serves 4, as a side

1 large lemon

350g frozen or fresh baby broad beans, *defrosted if frozen and skins removed*

2 baby gem lettuces, *core removed and leaves separated*

10g picked tarragon leaves

10g picked mint leaves

10g picked dill leaves

3 tbsp olive oil

100g toum *(p. 190)*

100g Greek-style yoghurt

salt and black pepper

1. Use a small, sharp knife to peel and segment the lemon. Roughly chop the segments into 3–4 pieces and put them into a large bowl, then squeeze what's left of the membrane into the bowl (you want about 1½ teaspoons of juice).

2. Add the broad beans, lettuce, herbs, 2 tablespoons of olive oil, ¼ teaspoon of salt and a good grind of pepper to the bowl of lemon and toss everything together well.

3. Mix together the toum and yoghurt, and spread out on a large platter. Top with the salad, slightly to one side. Drizzle all over with the remaining tablespoon of olive oil and serve.

Make it your own:
- Veganise it: use a dairy-free alternative for the yoghurt.
- Use defrosted peas in place of the broad beans, and any mixture of herbs and leaves you have on hand.

_____

_____

_____

(That one bag of) mixed veggies and potato fritters with harissa

Prep time: *25 minutes*
Cook time: *1 hour 20 minutes*
Chilling time: *30 minutes*

This fritter is inspired by Moroccan maakouda – a street-side snack of fried potato cakes, usually stuffed into a sandwich with plenty of harissa. This version utilises that one bag of frozen mixed veggies sitting in the back of your freezer, and bypasses the sandwich route altogether (although you could, by all means, go in that direction!). Serve these hot or at room temperature; they won't be as crispy once they've been sitting for a bit, but they will still taste wonderful.

Makes 16 fritters

2 baking potatoes, *peeled and cut into 3cm chunks (500g)*
250g frozen mixed vegetables, *steamed according to packet directions and drained*
2 garlic cloves, *roughly chopped*
10g parsley, *roughly chopped*
2½ tsp cumin seeds, *toasted and roughly crushed with a pestle and mortar*
1 egg
2 tsp finely grated lemon zest
30g plain flour
700ml sunflower oil, *for deep-frying*
salt and black pepper

BATTER
85g plain flour
40g cornflour
1¼ tsp fast-action dried yeast, *or 12g fresh yeast roughly crumbled*
⅔ tsp baking powder
⅔ tsp ground turmeric
145ml lukewarm water

HARISSA DIP
1½ tbsp rose harissa
2 tbsp lemon juice
1½ tsp runny honey
2 garlic cloves, *crushed*
2 tbsp olive oil

1. Put the potatoes and 2 teaspoons of salt into a medium saucepan, for which you have a lid, and add enough water to cover by about 3cm. Bring to the boil on a medium-high heat, then lower the heat to medium, cover, and cook for 8 minutes, or until easily pierced with a knife. Drain well, then, when cool enough to handle, use a potato ricer to rice the potatoes into a large bowl.

2. While the potatoes are cooking, put the steamed mixed vegetables, garlic and parsley into a food processor and pulse a few times until everything is finely chopped. Add to the bowl of potatoes along with the cumin, egg, lemon zest, 1 teaspoon of salt and a good grind of pepper. Mix to combine, then refrigerate for 30 minutes, to firm up slightly.

3. Make the dip by whisking together all the ingredients in a small bowl with a tiny pinch of salt.

4. Make the batter by whisking together all the ingredients with ⅓ teaspoon of salt in a medium bowl. Set aside to bubble up for about 20 minutes.

5. Meanwhile, put the 30g of flour into a shallow bowl. Use your hands to form 40–45g patties (about 5cm in diameter) of the potato mixture and dip each one into the flour to coat, shaking off the excess. You should make about 16 patties – don't worry if they're not perfect.

6. Heat the sunflower oil in a medium, high-sided sauté pan over a medium-high heat. Test it is hot by dropping a bit of batter into the oil – it should sizzle almost immediately. Working one at a time, dip each potato patty into the batter to coat, then drop it into the hot oil (don't worry if there are scraggly bits of batter – this adds to the look). Fry 6–7 at a time, for about 6–7 minutes, or until deeply golden. Use a slotted spoon to transfer them to a tray lined with kitchen paper, sprinkle with a little salt, and continue with the rest.

7. Transfer the fritters to a serving plate and serve the harissa dip in a bowl alongside.

Make it your own:

- Serve with yoghurt instead of the harissa dip to make this kid-friendly.
- Use up other frozen vegetables, such as peas or broccoli.
- Leave out the yeast if you can't get any.

_____

_____

_____

Creamed corn stuffed peppers with pickled jalapeños

Prep time: *20 minutes*
Cook time: *1 hour 15 minutes*

These impressive-looking peppers are deceptively easy to put together, and a sure way to put that bag of frozen sweetcorn to good use. Eat this alongside the broad bean and herb salad (p. 195) or some roasted potatoes, for a complete meal.

Serves 4, as a light lunch

1 green jalapeño, *thinly sliced, seeds and all (15g)*

2 tbsp apple cider vinegar

1 tsp caster sugar

250g frozen sweetcorn kernels, *defrosted*

100ml double cream

50g quick-cook polenta

3 garlic cloves, *crushed*

1 egg

105ml olive oil

75g low-moisture mozzarella, *roughly grated*

75g mature cheddar, *roughly grated*

4 medium red romano peppers

2 onions, *cut into 5 x 1cm rounds*

5g thyme sprigs

10g fresh coriander, *finely chopped*

salt and black pepper

1. Preheat the oven to 180°C fan.

2. Put the jalapeño, vinegar and sugar into a small bowl and mix to combine. Set aside to pickle.

3. Put the sweetcorn, cream, polenta, two-thirds of the garlic, the egg, 1 tablespoon of oil, ¾ teaspoon of salt and a generous grind of pepper into a food processor and pulse to a very rough purée. Transfer to a bowl and stir through the cheeses.

4. Use a small, sharp knife to make an incision lengthways into each romano pepper (making sure not to cut through the ends), keeping the stem intact. Gently use your fingers to remove and discard the seeds, then stuff each pepper with the sweetcorn mixture.

5. Put 1 tablespoon of oil in the base of a large, cast-iron saucepan or sauté pan and then top with the onion rounds and thyme to cover the base, sprinkling with a little salt and pepper. Place the peppers, slit side up, on top of the onions and drizzle them with 1 tablespoon of oil. Season lightly with salt and pepper, then pour 200ml of water into the pan, making sure not to pour it on top of the peppers. Bake for 30 minutes, then turn the heat up to 200°C fan and bake for another 20 minutes, or until everything is soft and nicely coloured.

6. Meanwhile, put the remaining 4 tablespoons of oil, the coriander, the remaining garlic, ⅛ teaspoon of salt and a good grind of pepper into a small bowl and stir to combine.

7. Spoon the coriander oil and pickled jalapeños over the peppers and serve warm.

Make it your own:
- Use regular red peppers if you can't find romano.
- Play with your cheeses – anything oozy and melty will work here!
- Double this recipe if cooking for a larger crowd.

Get ahead:
- Prepare and stuff the peppers a day ahead, ready to be baked on the day.

Greens and chermoula potato pie

Prep time: *30 minutes*
Cook time: *1 hour
25 minutes*
Chilling time: *20 minutes +*

We're constantly feeding off each other's vibes at the OTK: someone will make a dish, setting off a series of inspirational takes out of which a number of new dishes are born. Verena came up with this pie, saying, 'I love how you savoury chefs use greens and herbs so liberally.' V obviously went one step further, making her own pastry like the true pastry chef that she is. We use store-bought puff here, but you can always take a page out of V's book and make your pastry, if you like.

Serves 4, generously

60ml olive oil

2 onions, *thinly sliced (360g)*

350g frozen spinach, *defrosted and drained of excess water*

15g dill, *roughly chopped*

1½ tsp finely grated lemon zest

1 frozen all-butter puff pastry sheet, *defrosted (325g)*

130g Greek feta, *roughly crumbled*

1 baking potato, *skin on and scrubbed clean, then very thinly sliced 1mm thick (250g)*

CHERMOULA

5 garlic cloves, *roughly chopped*

1 red chilli, *roughly chopped, seeds and all (10g)*

2 tsp cumin seeds, *toasted and roughly crushed with a pestle and mortar*

1 tsp paprika

30g fresh coriander, *roughly chopped*

60ml olive oil

1½ tbsp lemon juice

salt and black pepper

1. For the chermoula, put the garlic, chilli, cumin, paprika, coriander, ½ teaspoon of salt, a good grind of pepper and 3 tablespoons of oil into a food processor and pulse into a coarse paste. Set aside.

2. Next, make the pie filling. Put 3 tablespoons of oil into a large sauté pan on a medium-high heat. Once the oil is hot, add the onions and cook, stirring occasionally, for about 12 minutes, or until softened and well browned. Add half the chermoula paste, the spinach, 1 teaspoon of salt and a good grind of pepper, and cook for 2–3 minutes more. Remove from the heat and add the dill and lemon zest. Set aside to cool, about 20 minutes.

3. Line a 24cm tart tin with a piece of baking parchment large enough to cover the base and a little bit over the sides (the excess will help you lift out the tart when it's baked). Lay the puff pastry on top, cutting away any excess overhang and using the extra pastry to fill any gaps. You want the pastry to evenly fit the base and sides of the tin.

4. Poke the base all over (about 10 times) with a fork, then spread the cooled spinach mixture over it evenly. Sprinkle over the feta, then roughly crimp the pastry edges to create a 2cm rim around the pie. Refrigerate the pie for at least 20 minutes – you want to bake it from cold.

5. Preheat the oven to 180°C fan.

6. Toss the potato together in a bowl with 1 tablespoon of oil, ½ teaspoon of salt and a good grind of pepper. Fan out the slices in a circular pattern, overlapping slightly, to cover the filling but not the pastry rim.

7. Bake the pie from cold for 45–50 minutes, or until cooked through and nicely coloured. Set aside to cool, about 15 minutes.

8. When ready to serve, stir the lemon juice and the remaining tablespoon of oil into the rest of the chermoula. Spoon half of this all over the pie, serving the remainder in a bowl alongside.

Make it your own:
- Swap out the frozen spinach for other greens such as kale or chard.
- Veganise it: leave out the feta and use vegan puff pastry for the base.

_____

_____

_____

Get ahead:
- Assemble the pie (minus the potato) a day ahead and keep refrigerated.

Skillet berries, bread and browned butter

Prep time: *15 minutes*
Cook time: *1 hour*

This is a great way to use up all the bits: a bag of frozen berries, those oats at the back of your pantry, that bread that really needs using up. The inspiration for this dish was the very British summer pudding, its simple combination of soft bread and berries winning the hearts of the nation. Like many of our dishes, it took a bit of a left-field turn and landed right here, in this cosy place of browned butter and oats, toasted sourdough and sweet spiced fruit. Serve this as a brunch dish or a late afternoon treat.

Serves 6

4 large Braeburn apples *(650g), peeled, cored and each cut into 6 wedges*

1½ tsp ground star anise, *plus an extra ¼ tsp to serve*

1½ tsp vanilla bean paste, *or vanilla extract*

130g unsalted butter

75g caster sugar

120g stale crustless sourdough, *roughly torn into 1cm pieces*

100g rolled oats

½ tsp flaked sea salt

500g frozen mixed berries, *kept frozen*

150ml double cream, *very cold*

1. Preheat the oven to 180°C fan.

2. Put the apples, ½ teaspoon of star anise, half the vanilla, 30g of butter and 30g of sugar into a large, ovenproof sauté pan. Transfer to the oven for to bake 20–25 minutes, stirring halfway through, or until the apples have softened but still retain their shape.

3. While the apples are baking, put the remaining 100g of butter into a large frying pan on a medium-high heat. Once melted, cook for 4–4½ minutes, swirling the pan often, or until nicely browned and nutty. Transfer the browned butter to a large bowl and return the pan to the heat. Add the sourdough and toast for 2 minutes, stirring often, then add to the browned-butter bowl.

Next, toast the oats in the same way for 2 minutes and add them to the bowl. Add the salt, the remaining teaspoon of star anise and the remaining 45g of sugar, and stir everything together well.

4. When the apples are ready, stir in the frozen berries and 2 tablespoons of water and top with the bread mixture. Turn the oven temperature down to 165°C fan and bake for 30 minutes, or until golden and bubbling. Leave to settle for about 5–10 minutes, then sprinkle with the extra star anise.

5. Combine the cold cream and the remaining vanilla in a small bowl. Serve the crumble warm, with the cold cream to drizzle on top.

Make it your own:

- Use whatever mixture of frozen or fresh berries you have on hand.
- Play with your spices and bread, using up what you have in your pantry.
- Make this super decadent and swap out the cold cream for vanilla ice cream.

_____

_____

At the very

END.

At the very end

At the very end . . . or at the very beginning – we won't hold it against you either way – when you're craving something sweet to balance out the salty, we've got you covered. Ixta, Noor and Chaya cook mostly savoury things, but that's not to say they don't delve into the world of sweet treats from time to time. Verena, on the other hand, with baking very much a part of her DNA, lives and breathes this world, speaking with the detailed precision of a chef who understands that 'baking and pastry' is, in fact, a science. To fully understand it – the whats, whys and hows – you must first wrap your mind around the delicate chemistry behind it (cue the chocoflan, p. 226).

We often joke that Noor and Ixta approach pastry with a much more 'wing it and see what happens' attitude. Verena watches them, amused, politely biting her tongue at the possible disasters that might ensue. There have been too many to count, really, the two savoury chefs frequently frustrated at their ongoing sugar-laced catastrophes. Interestingly enough, their headstrong approach often works, exploring flavour combinations and methods that might be slightly radical (see cheesy fruity stromboli, funky faloodeh or sticky miso bananas on pp. 232, 215 and 240 respectively). The point being that, at the Test Kitchen, baking is one part science and two parts sheer determination.

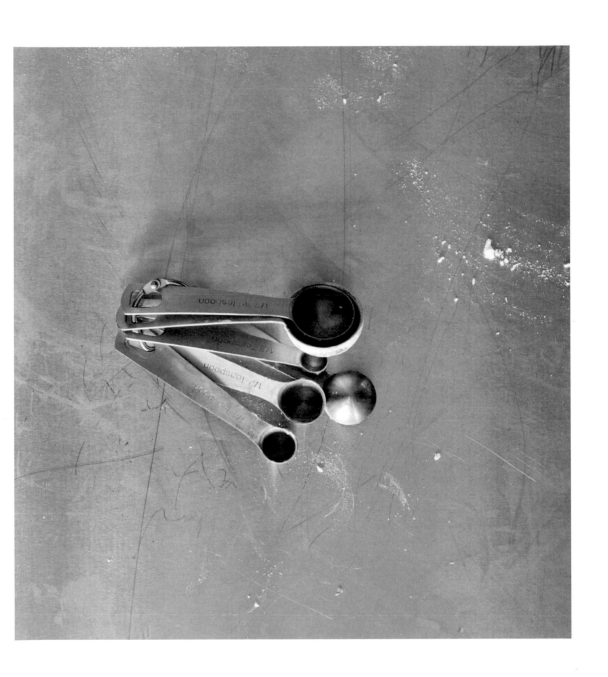

Carrot cake sandwich cookies

Prep time: *20 minutes*
Cook time: *1 hour*

These cookies are more cake than cookie, like a carrot cake in bite size. Not dissimilar to an American whoopie pie, you could say.

There's a significant amount of science involved in cookie making, despite what the Cookie Monster will have you believe. They can be temperamental at the best of times, really, so do make sure you follow these steps to ensure happy sandwich cookies and happy bellies all around. Don't over-whip the butter and cream cheese, for example, make sure they're softened at room temperature, and make sure that the cookies are nicely spread out on your tray before baking too.

Makes 15 sandwich cookies

CARROT CAKE

250g plain flour

1¼ tsp bicarbonate of soda

1 tsp baking powder

1½ tsp ground cinnamon

1 tsp ground ginger

¼ tsp ground cloves

½ tsp salt

100g pecans, *toasted and finely chopped*

30g desiccated coconut

300g finely grated carrots *(from about 3 carrots)*

120g unsalted butter, *softened at room temperature*

100g light soft brown sugar

100g caster sugar

2 large eggs

2 tsp vanilla bean paste

80g sultanas

CREAM CHEESE FILLING

90g unsalted butter, *softened at room temperature*

125g icing sugar, *sifted, plus 2 tsp extra for dusting*

225g full-fat cream cheese, *at room temperature*

2½ tsp finely grated orange zest

1. Preheat the oven to 180°C fan. Line two large baking trays with baking parchment.

2. In a large bowl, whisk together the flour, bicarbonate of soda, baking powder, spices, salt, pecans and coconut. Set aside.

3. Use your hands to squeeze out as much liquid as possible from the carrots – you want 200g of grated carrot after it has been wrung out.

4. Put the butter and both sugars into the bowl of a stand mixer, with the paddle attachment in place, and beat on medium speed for 90 seconds, until just combined. Add the eggs, one at a time, then, once incorporated, add the vanilla, carrots and sultanas and mix to combine. Turn the speed to low and gradually add the dry ingredients, mixing until just incorporated. Clean the mixer bowl and paddle attachment to use later.

5. Transfer the mixture to a piping bag and snip the end to make an opening about 2½cm wide. Pipe heaped tablespoons of the mixture, about 35g in weight and 5–6cm in diameter, on to your prepared baking trays, using your fingers to round them off slightly (don't flatten them). Bake for 10 minutes, or until just cooked through but soft to the touch. Leave to cool slightly before gently transferring them to a wire rack to cool completely. Repeat to make 30 cookies in total.

Get ahead:
- Make the cookies and filling separately up to 2 days ahead. Store the cookies in an airtight container and keep the filling refrigerated. Assemble when ready to serve.

6. Meanwhile, make the filling. Beat the butter and icing sugar together in the bowl of the stand mixer, with the paddle attachment in place, on medium speed for 5 minutes, until very light and fluffy. Measure out the cream cheese in a separate small bowl and mix briefly with a spatula until smooth. Add to the creamed butter and icing sugar, along with the orange zest, and beat until just combined. Chill for 10 minutes to firm up a little before using.

7. Once the cookies have cooled, pair them up – trying to match similar sizes. Spoon a generous tablespoon of the cream cheese filling on to the flat side of one cookie. Top with the flat side of the other cookie to make a sandwich. Repeat to give you 15 sandwiches in total. Dust the tops of the cookies with the extra icing sugar and serve on the same day.

Make it your own:

– Use lemon juice instead of the lime, and raspberry or strawberry
  purée in place of the pomegranate syrup.

_____

_____

Funky faloodeh

Prep time: *15 minutes*
Cook time: *1 hour*
Freezing time: *6 hours to overnight*

Faloodeh is a popular Persian dessert made up of cold vermicelli noodles mixed with frozen granita or ice cream, and comes in many different forms and flavours. It might seem a little strange to those unaccustomed to noodles for dessert, but trust us: it is cold, sweet and refreshing and just what's needed on a hot summer day. It's also super quirky and fun to make (and to look at)! Make sure that all your components are set and, once you're ready, put them together quickly and only just before serving.

Serves 6

220g caster sugar

20g mint sprigs

150 lime juice

100g dried vermicelli rice noodles *(we use Thai Taste)*

POMEGRANATE SYRUP

200ml pomegranate juice *(unsweetened)*

1 tbsp caster sugar

1½ tsp good-quality rose water

TO SERVE

3 tbsp pomegranate seeds

1 large lime: *finely grate the zest to get 1½ tsp and then cut into 6 wedges*

1. Put the sugar, 300ml of water and the mint into a medium saucepan on a medium-high heat. Bring to a simmer, stirring to dissolve the sugar, then add the lime juice and set aside to cool completely.

2. Strain the mixture through a sieve into a freezer-proof container, discarding the solids, then cover and freeze for about 2 hours. Use a fork to scrape at the half-frozen mixture, then return to the freezer and continue in this way, scraping at the mixture every half hour or so, for a total of 4 hours.

3. Cook the noodles in plenty of boiling water for 6 minutes, or until very soft (you want to overcook them slightly). Drain well, then use a pair of kitchen scissors to cut the noodles roughly in half.

4. Make the pomegranate syrup by putting the juice and sugar into a medium saucepan and placing it on a medium heat. Cook for 20–25 minutes, until reduced to the consistency of

maple syrup. Stir in the rose water and set aside to cool.

5. When you are nearly ready to serve the faloodeh, fill a large bowl with cold water and plenty of ice and add the cooked vermicelli noodles. Refrigerate for about 15 minutes.

6. Remove the lime granita from the fridge about 5–10 minutes before you want to serve it, scraping at it with a fork to get that snowflake effect.

7. Working quickly, drain the noodles well in a sieve, wipe out the bowl, then return the noodles to the bowl along with half the granita and toss to combine. Some of the noodles will start to solidify a little (that's what you want). Divide the mixture between six small bowls or martini glasses, and top with the remaining granita. Add a spoonful of the pomegranate syrup to each bowl, then sprinkle with the pomegranate seeds and lime zest. Serve each bowl with a lime wedge to squeeze on top.

> **Get ahead:**
> – Make the syrup, cooked noodles and frozen granita the day before.

Coconut dream cake

Prep time: *15 minutes*
Cook time: *1 hour 20 minutes
to 1 hour 50 minutes*

Yotam and Noor had differing opinions when it came to this cake. Yotam, team one-layer, and Noor, team two-layers, because why have one when you can have two? Verena soon came into the conversation and swiftly voted for team two-layers (much to Noor's delight), but although there was a clear winner, we've decided to let you take charge – the cake can be baked in two 20cm round cake tins, creating that 'sandwich' effect, or one large rectangular one. Either way, this cake is an absolute dream (because surely dreams are laced with coconut, cardamom and sugar). Double or triple up on the coconut topping here – it's ridiculously delicious snacking material.

Serves 8

320g self-raising flour

15 cardamom pods, *shells discarded and seeds roughly crushed with a pestle and mortar*

½ tsp bicarbonate of soda

½ tsp salt

300g caster sugar

170g unsalted butter, *softened at room temperature, then roughly cut into 3cm cubes, plus extra for greasing*

5 egg whites, *at room temperature*

120g Greek-style yoghurt, *at room temperature*

1 tbsp vanilla bean paste, *or the seeds scraped from 1 vanilla pod*

240ml full-fat coconut milk

COCONUT FROSTING

200g unsalted butter, *softened at room temperature, then roughly cut into 3cm cubes*

150g icing sugar, *sifted*

150g full-fat cream cheese, *at room temperature*

COCONUT TOPPING

100g coconut flakes *(aka coconut chips)*

3 tbsp maple syrup

10 cardamom pods, *shells discarded and seeds roughly crushed with a pestle and mortar*

¼ tsp salt

Get ahead:

– Make the topping up to 3 days ahead and keep it sealed in an airtight container.

– Bake the cakes a day ahead, wrap them well and assemble the next day.

---

1. Preheat the oven to 165°C fan. Grease and use baking parchment to line the base and sides of a 20cm round springform cake tin (or two if you have more than one tin) or a rectangular baking tin measuring 33cm x 23cm and 4cm deep.

2. Put the flour, cardamom, bicarbonate of soda and salt into a large bowl and whisk together to combine.

3. Put the caster sugar and butter into the bowl of a stand mixer, with the paddle attachment in place, and beat on medium-high speed until light and fluffy, about 4 minutes. Scrape down the sides of the bowl, turn the speed to medium and add the egg whites, mixing to just incorporate, then add the yoghurt and vanilla bean paste and beat for 30 seconds. Scrape down the sides of the bowl and turn the speed down to low. Add a third of the flour mixture and a third of the coconut milk, alternating until both are combined and the mixture is smooth.

4. Team two-layers: Transfer half the mixture, about 630g, to the prepared tin and bake for 35 minutes, or until a skewer inserted into the centre comes out clean. Set aside to cool slightly before very carefully releasing it from its tin and inverting it on to a cake stand or plate. Line the tin again and bake the remaining half in the same way, leaving both to cool completely.

5. Team one-layer: Transfer the mixture to your prepared rectangular baking tin and bake for 35 minutes, or until a skewer inserted into the centre comes out clean. Set aside to cool completely.

6. Meanwhile, make the topping by putting the coconut flakes, maple syrup, cardamom and salt on a parchment-lined baking tray and tossing to combine. Bake for 8 minutes, give everything a good stir, then bake for 5 minutes more, or until nicely browned and crispy. Set aside to cool and crisp up further.

7. Once the cakes have cooled, make the frosting. Add the butter and sugar to the stand mixer, with the paddle attachment in place, and beat on medium-high speed until light and creamy, about 5 minutes. Beat the cream cheese in a bowl until smooth, then add to the stand mixer with the creamed butter and mix on medium-low until just combined and no longer streaky.

8. Team two-layers: Spread a little less than half the frosting on the inverted cake, spreading to cover the top. Release the second cake from its tin (if you haven't already) and gently invert on top, so that the bottom is now the top. Spread the remaining icing around the top and sides of the cake, using an offset spatula to help you. Don't worry if it looks a little messy; this is all part of its charm. Lastly top with the coconut topping so that it covers the top of the cake, leaving the sides exposed.

9. Team one-layer: Spread the frosting all over the top of the cake, creating little grooves and waves with your spatula. Top with the coconut topping.

10. Refrigerate if not serving right away, adding the coconut topping just before serving.

Upside-down lemon, maple and vanilla pudding with lemon-maple butter

Prep time: *15 minutes*
Cook time: *1 hour 40 minutes*

This magnificent pudding was made with the purpose of showcasing winter lemons, their bitter flesh a great way to cut through an otherwise decadent eating experience. As happy accidents go, this was tested alongside a separate dish which included a maple-butter sauce. A squeeze of lemon and a generous amount of maple butter was spooned over the pudding because well, why not, and it suddenly dawned on us that lemon-maple butter had been the missing component all along. Lesson learned: sometimes that which is very, very wrong can turn out to be really quite right.

Be sure to remove the butter for the pudding from the fridge well in advance – it needs to be super softened at room temperature before making the base.

Serves 8

3 medium lemons, *thinly sliced into ¼cm-thick rounds to get 24 slices, pips removed*

165ml maple syrup

1 vanilla pod, *halved lengthways, seeds scraped and reserved with the pod*

225g plain flour

2 tsp baking powder

⅓ tsp salt

225g unsalted butter, *softened at room temperature, then cut into 2cm cubes*

3 large eggs, *plus 1 yolk*

225g light soft brown sugar

60ml whole milk

240g crème fraîche, *to serve*

1. Preheat the oven to 170°C fan. Line a baking dish about 30cm x 20cm in size with a piece of baking parchment large enough to cover the base and sides, with enough overhang to fold over the pudding as well.

2. Place a large, non-stick frying pan on a high heat and, once very hot, char a third of the lemon slices on both sides – about 1–2 minutes per side. Continue in this way with the rest.

3. Put 120ml of maple syrup and the scraped-out vanilla pod in the base of your prepared baking dish. Top with the charred lemon slices, spreading out so they cover the entire base, overlapping in places.

4. Sift the flour, baking powder and salt into the bowl of a stand mixer, with the whisk attachment in place, and mix on medium speed to combine. Add the softened butter, eggs, yolk, vanilla seeds, brown sugar, milk and the remaining 3 tablespoons of maple syrup, and mix on medium speed for 2 minutes until combined. The mixture will look as if it's split a little with some smaller cubes of butter – but that's okay.

5. Spoon the mixture into a piping bag, snipping the base, and pipe the mixture evenly on top of the lemons in the baking dish (piping the mixture ensures the lemons don't move around too much). Gently smooth over the mixture with the back of a spoon. Fold over the excess baking parchment to cover, then wrap the dish tightly in foil.

LEMON-MAPLE BUTTER

50ml lemon juice

120ml maple syrup

120g unsalted butter,
*fridge cold and cut into
1½cm cubes*

6. Place the baking dish in a larger roasting tin (roughly 40cm x 28cm). Pour enough boiling water into the tin to come 3cm up the sides (about 1 litre), then bake for 70 minutes, or until a toothpick inserted into the centre comes out clean. Remove the foil, unwrap the top of the pudding and lift out the baking dish from the water. Set aside for 5 minutes before carefully inverting the whole thing on to a platter, removing the parchment paper to expose the lemons.

7. Towards the last 10 minutes of cooking, make the lemon-maple butter. Put the lemon juice and maple syrup into a small saucepan and bring to a simmer on a medium-high heat. Cook for about 2 minutes, then turn the heat down to low and, when no longer simmering, gradually add the butter cubes a little at a time, whisking with each addition until incorporated. Don't let the mixture boil at all – you should be left with an emulsified sauce. Remove from the heat.

8. Drizzle one-third of the lemon-maple butter all over the pudding and serve warm, with the extra maple butter and crème fraîche alongside.

Make it your own:
– Try this recipe using kumquats instead of lemons and orange juice instead of lemon juice.

Make it your own:
- Use any frozen berries you like, or mix it up by adding some frozen mango or banana.
- Go crazy with your choice of toppings: nuts, fruits and any type of chocolate shavings!

_____

_____

_____

Frozen berries for little humans

Prep time: *10 minutes*
Cook time: *5 minutes*
Freezing time: *30–40 minutes*

Bags of frozen berries are a sure way to quick-fix a sweet craving. This recipe is courtesy of our colleague Claudine Boulstridge, who is always on the lookout for creative ways to feed her three kids, and to keep the options healthy . . . ish. A great one for the little humans, but the adults sort of (really!) like it too.

Serves 4 little humans

350g frozen raspberries,
kept frozen
140ml double cream,
fridge cold
1 tbsp vanilla bean paste,
*or the scraped seeds of
1 vanilla pod*
30g icing sugar
**2 tbsp pomegranate
molasses**

TOPPING
40g white chocolate,
*peeled with a vegetable
peeler to make curls*
30g coconut flakes, *well
toasted*

1. Put all the ingredients, except the chocolate and coconut flakes, into a food processor and blitz until completely smooth, scraping down the sides of the bowl as needed. Transfer to a freezer-proof container, for which you have a lid, cover and transfer to the freezer for just 30–40 minutes (you want it to be a loose, soft-serve consistency).

2. Scoop into four small bowls and sprinkle with the white chocolate and coconut flakes.

Verena's road trip cookies

Prep time: *10 minutes*
Cook time: *1 hour 15 minutes*
Chilling time: *2 hours to overnight*

A few members of the OTK gang took a road trip to Durdle Door – 'a nice road trip out of London', said Verena, but it was more to satisfy Noor's constant quest for sunshine. Gitai soon took charge of the music, and off to the beach they went. Halfway through the journey, the mid-morning munchies kicked in and Verena whipped out a box of her homemade oatmeal cookies, baked fresh that morning. They smelt of cinnamon and hugs, were the perfect ratio of chewy to soft, and, beyond anything, it was V's cookies that made the trip so wonderfully sweet.

Makes 28 cookies

275g unsalted butter, *cut into 2cm cubes, at room temperature*
175g light soft brown sugar
75g caster sugar
20g vanilla bean paste, *or vanilla extract*
180g jumbo rolled oats
155g oat bran
100g plain flour
1 tsp ground cinnamon
¾ tsp freshly grated nutmeg
¼ tsp baking powder
1 tsp bicarbonate of soda
1 tsp salt
200g raisins or sultanas *(or a mix)*
1 egg

1. Put 75g of the butter, both sugars and the vanilla into a large bowl, mix to combine and set aside.

2. Put the jumbo oats, oat bran, plain flour, cinnamon, nutmeg, baking powder, bicarbonate of soda, salt and raisins (or sultanas) into a separate large bowl and mix together to combine.

3. Put the remaining 200g of butter into a medium saucepan on a medium heat and leave to melt and bubble away, whisking every now and then. As the butter browns, it will begin to foam, colour and smell nutty – keep whisking and, once it turns deeply brown, remove from the heat, about 6–7 minutes in total. Immediately pour the browned butter into the bowl containing the cubed butter and sugars and whisk until combined (it will look separated with the butter sitting on top, but that's okay).

4. Set aside for 10 minutes to cool slightly, stirring once or twice. Add the egg and whisk until combined. Next add the contents of the jumbo oats bowl and use a spatula to mix into a soft dough. Cover the surface of the dough and transfer to the fridge to rest and firm up for 2 hours, or overnight. If the latter, remove from the fridge about an hour before baking.

5. Preheat the oven to 180°C fan. Roll the dough into 28 balls, each roughly 40g in weight, and transfer 6–8 balls, well spaced apart, to a large parchment-lined baking tray.

6. Bake each batch of cookies for 7 minutes, then rotate the tray and bake for 4–5 minutes more. The cookies will have set and lightly browned around the edges and will look puffy and under-baked in the middle. Leave each batch to cool for about 15 minutes before eating them warm, or devouring them later at room temperature.

Get ahead:
- Store any extra baked cookies in an airtight container – they will keep for up to 2 days (if they last that long).
- Keep any unbaked cookie dough in the fridge for up to 3 days, baking as you need.

Chocoflan

Prep time: *10 minutes*
Cook time: *1 hour 20 minutes*
Cooling time: *3 hours to overnight*

'So bad, it's good' couldn't be more fitting than for chocoflan, a dessert which combines two layers of pure decadence into one cake (think brownie meets flan). There's also a nifty science trick involved, where the cake layer and flan layer swap positions during the baking, adding to the kitchen wizardry. We've tested this using different tins, without much success, so do make sure you use a 27cm bundt tin that does not have a removable base.

Serves 10–12

160g caramel sauce
(thick set), store-bought or homemade (we used Waitrose salted caramel dipping sauce)

1 tbsp whole milk

CHOCOLATE CAKE

250g plain flour

½ tsp baking powder

½ tsp bicarbonate of soda

70g cocoa powder

¼ tsp salt

120g unsalted butter,
softened at room temperature, plus extra for greasing

100g dark muscovado sugar

125g caster sugar

2 large eggs

200ml buttermilk *(220g)*

FLAN

1 tin of evaporated milk *(400g)*

1 tin of sweetened condensed milk *(397g)*

120g full-fat cream cheese,
at room temperature

3 large eggs

2 tsp vanilla bean paste,
or vanilla extract

¼ tsp salt

1. Preheat the oven to 160°C fan. Liberally grease a 27cm bundt tin with butter, then coat the bottom with half the caramel sauce. Place the bundt tin in a larger roasting tin about 40cm x 28cm in size and set aside.

2. For the cake batter, sift the flour, baking powder, bicarbonate of soda, cocoa powder and salt into a medium bowl. Put the butter and both sugars into the bowl of a stand mixer with the paddle attachment in place. Beat on medium speed until light and fluffy, about 2 minutes. Add the eggs one at a time and beat until just incorporated, then turn the speed to medium-low. Add a third of the flour mixture and half the buttermilk and continue in this way, ending with the flour. Mix until everything is just incorporated, then transfer to the bundt tin, smoothing the batter evenly with the back of a spoon.

3. For the flan batter, put all the ingredients into a blender and blitz until smooth. Pour the flan batter over the cake batter, then cover the bundt tin with a circular piece of baking parchment, followed by a piece of foil, and wrap tightly. Add enough boiling water to the roasting tin to come about 2cm up the sides of the bundt tin. Transfer to the oven and bake for 1 hour, rotating halfway through, or until a skewer inserted into the cake comes out almost clean. Remove from the water bath, removing the foil and baking parchment, and leave to cool for about an hour (it won't be completely cool).

4. Invert the chocoflan on to a large round serving platter, shaking it slightly to release it from the tin, and refrigerate until completely cool, at least 2 hours or (preferably) overnight.

5. To serve, thin out the remaining 80g of caramel with the tablespoon of milk and drizzle all over the flan.

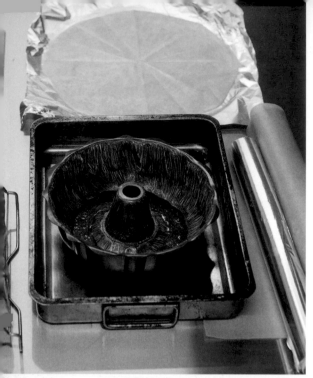

Get ahead:

– We really recommend
making this the day before.
It tastes best when it's
fridge cold, and the flavours
develop as it sits.

Muhallabieh with burnt honey orange syrup, kataifi and pistachio sugar

Prep time: *10 minutes*
Cook time: *45 minutes*
Setting time: *3 hours to overnight*

Like two siblings, Gitai and Noor often bicker, and in this case, over the name of this dessert – Gitai insists on calling it 'malabi', to which Noor rolls her eyes and says 'muhallabieh'. Either way, it's one and the same – the Middle Eastern equivalent of panna cotta, using rice or cornflour to set the creamy base. This version uses a bitter orange syrup and crispy kataifi to give it the texture and tang it needs. You can find kataifi in any Middle Eastern grocery store, but roughly broken filo pastry would work here too.

Serves 6

500ml whole milk

200ml double cream

50g caster sugar

¼ tsp flaked salt

50g cornflour

1 tsp good-quality orange
  blossom water

KATAIFI

60g kataifi, *defrosted if frozen*

25g unsalted butter, *melted*

1 tbsp olive oil

30g pistachios, *very lightly toasted*

1 tbsp caster sugar

¼ tsp flaked salt

BURNT HONEY ORANGE SYRUP

120g runny honey

2 oranges: *1 squeezed to get 60ml juice and the other peeled and segmented*

1. Make sure to have six small glass bowls or glasses at the ready. Put the milk, cream, sugar and salt into a medium saucepan and bring to a gentle simmer on a medium heat.

2. In a medium bowl whisk together the cornflour and 130ml of water until smooth. Once the milk mixture has come to a simmer, slowly add the cornflour mixture, whisking until smooth and similar in consistency to a thick custard, about 2 minutes. Stir in the orange blossom water and quickly pour the mixture into a jug, then divide it between your glasses or bowls. Cover the tops with a piece of baking parchment or cling film to stop any skin from forming. Leave to cool down slightly, then transfer to the fridge to set, at least 3 hours, or overnight if you're getting ahead.

3. Preheat the oven to 180°C fan. Put the kataifi, butter and oil into a bowl and toss to coat the strands. Using your fingers, gather about 10g of the strands and tightly wrap them around your index finger, to create a sort of messy 'bundle'. Transfer

to a small, parchment-lined baking tray and continue to make bundles, six in total. Bake for 12–15 minutes, until deeply golden and cooked through.

4. Put the pistachios, sugar and salt into the small bowl of a food processor and pulse until very finely chopped. Once cool, toss the kataifi bundles with two-thirds of the pistachio sugar (don't worry if they break apart a little).

5. Meanwhile, make the syrup by putting the honey into a small saucepan on a medium-high heat. Cook for 8–9 minutes, swirling the pan occasionally, until the honey turns a deep brown (don't be afraid to take it to the edge). Remove from the heat and add the orange juice. Set aside to cool. Roughly cut the orange segments into 3–4 pieces and add them to the syrup.

6. When ready to serve, remove the baking parchment (or cling film) and top the muhallabieh with the syrup, a kataifi bundle and a sprinkling of extra pistachio sugar. Serve cold.

Get ahead:

– Make the muhallabieh up to 2 days ahead, keeping them covered and refrigerated.
– Make the kataifi bundles up to 2 days ahead, keeping them in a well-sealed container.

Cheesy fruity stromboli

Prep time: *20 minutes*
Cook time: *1 hour 40 minutes*
Proving time: *1 hour*

Stromboli is basically a large piece of pizza dough that is rolled and stuffed with stuff. This fruity version straddles the line between sweet and savoury, and is ideal for brunch or a late afternoon treat. This stromboli is best eaten fresh, on the day it is baked.

Serves 6

DOUGH

190g plain flour

10g fresh yeast, *roughly crumbled, or 1½ tsp fast-action dried yeast*

1½ tsp caster sugar

⅔ tsp salt

1½ tbsp olive oil, *plus extra for oiling*

110ml lukewarm water

FILLING

3 small peaches *(350g), pitted and each cut into 6 wedges (300g)*

130g caster sugar

1½ tbsp olive oil

150g fresh blueberries

1½ tbsp cornflour

80g whole-milk ricotta

120g low-moisture mozzarella, *roughly grated*

2 tsp lemon zest

½ tbsp picked thyme leaves, *plus some extra soft sprigs*

1 egg yolk

1 tbsp demerara sugar

1. Preheat the oven to 200°C fan.

2. Put all the dough ingredients into the bowl of a stand mixer with the dough hook in place. Beat on medium-high speed for 8 minutes, or until the dough is smooth (it will be a little sticky). Use oiled hands to transfer the dough to a lightly oiled, large bowl and cover with a damp tea towel. Leave to double in size in a warm place, about an hour.

3. Meanwhile, put the peaches, 100g of caster sugar and the oil into a baking dish roughly 30cm x 20cm in size. Toss everything together and bake for 10 minutes. Add the blueberries and bake for 10 minutes more, or until the fruit has roasted and softened but still retains its shape. When cool, gently drain the mixture in a sieve set over a bowl, saving the liquid and the fruit. Put the fruit back into the baking dish and gently stir in 1 tablespoon of cornflour.

4. Put the fruit liquid into a small sauté pan and place it on a medium-high heat. Cook for 6–8 minutes, stirring occasionally, until reduced to a loose syrup. Set aside to cool and thicken.

5. Add the ricotta, mozzarella, lemon zest, the remaining ½ tablespoon of cornflour and the remaining 30g of caster sugar to a bowl and mix well to combine.

6. Line a large baking tray with baking parchment. Using well-oiled hands, transfer the dough to the lined tray and gently stretch it out so it's about 20cm x 28cm in size.

7. Spread the dough all over with the ricotta mixture, leaving a 2cm border around the outside.

8. Spoon over the fruit mixture, leaving a 4cm border around the outside. Sprinkle evenly with the picked thyme leaves.

9. With the longer end facing you, very gently pull over the dough to roll the stromboli into a long cylinder shape, pushing the fruit filling inwards and making it as compact as possible. Don't worry if you have a couple of small tears.

10. Arrange the thyme sprigs artfully on top, pushing them into the dough very gently, then brush with the egg yolk and sprinkle the top with the demerara sugar.

11. Bake for 10 minutes, then turn the heat down to 165°C fan and bake for 25 minutes more, until golden brown and cooked through. Remove from the oven and carefully transfer the stromboli to a wire rack. Leave to cool for about 20 minutes before serving, warm or at room temperature, with the fruit syrup alongside.

Make it your own:

- Save time and use shop-bought pizza dough instead.
- Use tinned peaches and frozen blueberries if you can't find in-season fresh ones.

Get ahead:

– Make the dough the day
ahead, leaving it to prove
in the fridge overnight.
Bring it back up to
room temerature before
working with it.

Almond, barberry and orange brittle with Aleppo chilli

Prep time: *25 minutes*
Cook time: *50 minutes*
Setting time: *1 hour 15 minutes*

This crunchy, sweet snack is dangerously moreish and a great way to use up all the nuts and seeds hanging out in your cupboards. This is a good one to serve as an afternoon treat.

Serves 8, as a snack

2 tbsp whipping cream

100g caster sugar

100g golden syrup

70g unsalted butter, *cut into roughly 3cm cubes*

1 tsp vanilla bean paste, *or vanilla extract*

1 tsp flaked sea salt

1 tsp Aleppo chilli, *or ½ tsp regular chilli flakes*

1 tsp good-quality orange blossom water

15g orange zest *(about 1½ tbsp finely grated zest, from 1–2 oranges)*

150g flaked almonds, *lightly toasted*

90g pecan or walnut pieces, *lightly toasted then finely chopped*

90g pumpkin seeds, *lightly toasted*

40g sesame seeds, *lightly toasted*

20g barberries, *soaked in 100ml boiling water for 10 minutes, then drained*

30g dark chocolate, *roughly chopped*

1. Preheat the oven to 145°C fan. Line a large, 40cm x 30cm baking tray with baking parchment.

2. Add the cream, sugar and golden syrup to a medium saucepan on a medium heat. Cook just until it starts to bubble, stirring occasionally, until it is very lightly golden and smooth. Remove from the heat, add the butter, vanilla, salt, chilli, orange blossom water and orange zest, and stir continuously until the butter has melted. Stir through the toasted nuts and seeds until well combined, then quickly transfer the mixture to your prepared baking tray. Use the back of a rubber spatula to spread out the mixture into a thin rectangle that covers the base of the tray.

3. Bake for 10 minutes, then rotate the tray and bake for 15 minutes more. Sprinkle evenly with the barberries, pushing them gently into the mix with the back of a spoon, and return to the oven for another 2 minutes. Set aside to cool completely, about 30–45 minutes.

4. Meanwhile, temper the chocolate. Put the chocolate into a heatproof bowl set over a small saucepan of simmering water, with the base of the bowl not touching the water. Once two-thirds melted, remove the bowl from the heat and gently stir until the chocolate is completely smooth and melted (this helps the chocolate set at room temperature).

5. Drizzle the melted chocolate all over the surface of the brittle, then leave to set completely, about 30 minutes, or refrigerate to help it set faster. Break the brittle apart into randomly-sized large pieces and serve piled on to a plate or board.

Make it your own:
– Play with your nuts and seeds, using more of less of either.
– Use other types of chocolate for drizzling.
– Bag and tie these up as a festive DIY gift!

_____

_____

_____

Get ahead:
– Store in an airtight container for up to a week.

Sticky miso bananas with lime and toasted rice

Prep time: *5 minutes*
Cook time: *30 minutes*

This dessert ticks all our flavour boxes – sweet, salty, tangy and umami – and all our texture boxes – sticky, crunchy and creamy. The bananas you use should have almost completely yellow skin, with only the tiniest bit of brown spotting.

Serves 4

40g unsalted butter
70g light soft brown sugar
½ tsp ground star anise
3 tbsp crème fraîche
1½ tbsp white miso
4 medium bananas *(medium ripe), peeled and halved lengthways*
1 lime: *finely grate the zest to get 1 tsp and then juice to get 1½ tsp*

TOASTED RICE TOPPING
1 tbsp Thai sticky rice *(raw), or jasmine rice*
2 tsp black sesame seeds
½ tsp ground star anise

1. Set the oven to its highest grill setting.

2. Make the topping. Toast the rice in a small frying pan on a medium heat for 12–15 minutes, shaking the pan from time to time, until deeply golden. Blitz in a spice or coffee grinder until fine, then transfer to a small bowl. Return the pan to a medium-high heat and add the sesame seeds. Toast for 1 minute, then stir into the rice bowl along with the star anise. Set aside.

3. Put the butter, sugar, star anise and half the crème fraîche into a large, ovenproof cast-iron pan (or a large sauté pan) on a medium heat. Stir the mixture frequently, until the butter has melted and the sugar has dissolved, then, off the heat, whisk in the miso until smooth. Add the bananas, cut side up, using a spoon to coat the tops with some of the caramel, then transfer to the oven and grill for about 8 minutes (this will vary, depending on your grill, so check them at the 7-minute mark), or until the bananas have softened and are lightly browned.

4. While the bananas are grilling, mix the remaining crème fraîche with the lime juice. When ready, spoon this all over the bananas, then sprinkle with the lime zest and a tablespoon of the rice topping. Serve immediately and directly from the pan, with the extra rice topping alongside.

Make it your own:
– No spice grinder? No problem! Swap out the ground rice for nuts, seeds or coconut flakes.

_____

_____

_____

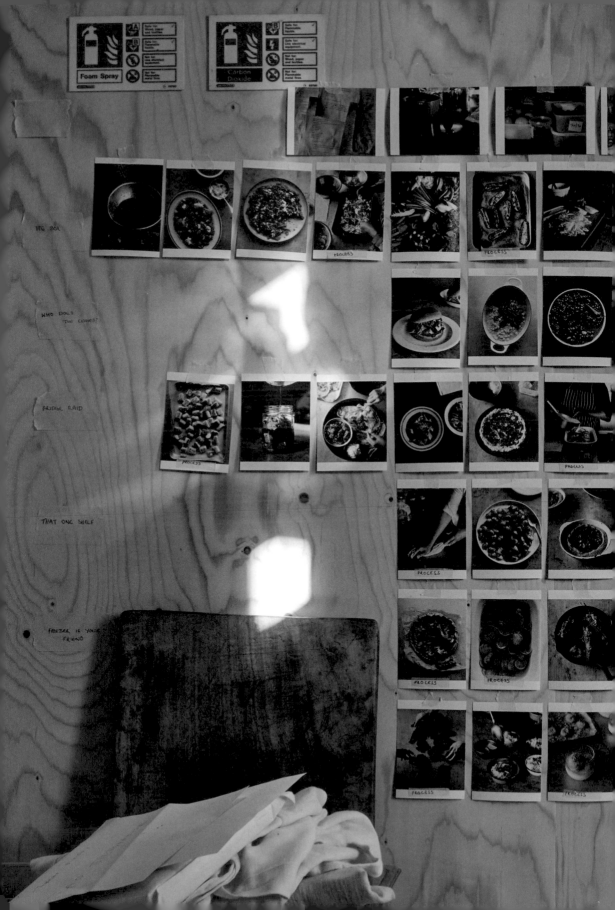

Index

star anise: soda bread with figs, star anise and orange **41**

sticky miso bananas with lime and toasted rice **240**

sticky sweet and sour plums and sausages **131**

strata: kale pesto strata with Gruyère and mustard **136–9**

stromboli, cheesy fruity **232–5**

sugar snap peas: crudités **64**

sultanas: carrot cake sandwich cookies **212–13**

    Verena's road trip cookies **224–5**

sumac: black lime beef skewers with sumac onions **52–3**

    gnocchi with sumac onions and brown butter pine nuts **170–3**

summer courgettes with tomatoes and ricotta **81**

swede: 5-a-day toad-in-the-hole **106–9**

sweet potato shakshuka with sriracha butter and pickled onions **84–5**

sweet spiced mushroom and rice pilaf **127**

sweetcorn: cobb salad with mango and lime dressing **184–7**

    creamed corn stuffed peppers with pickled jalapeños **199**

    spiced semolina with sweetcorn, peanuts and coriander **59**

Swiss chard: tamarind, greens and mung beans with turmeric oil **38–9**

syrup, black lime honey **54**

T

tabbouleh fritters with quick chilli sauce **56**

tahini: burnt aubergine, tomato and tahini **83**

    creamy dreamy hummus **20**

    green cannellini and tahini **27**

    Ixta's biang biang noodles **44–7**

    peas, tahini and za'atar **182**

    smoky, creamy pasta with burnt aubergine and tahini **146–7**

    za'atar salmon and tahini **119**

tamarind, greens and mung beans with turmeric oil **38–9**

tandoori chickpeas, confit **105**

(that one bag of) mixed veggies and potato fritters with harissa **196–7**

toad-in-the-hole, 5-a-day **106–9**

tomatoes: baked orzo puttanesca **114**

    braised green beans with tomato, cardamom and garlic **188–9**

    burnt aubergine, tomato and tahini **83**

    charred tomatoes, onions and peppers with feta and harissa pine nuts **128**

    cheesy polenta and tomato sauce **24**

    confit tandoori chickpeas **105**

    cream of tomato soup with buttery onions and orecchiette **169**

    fish koftas in ancho chilli and tomato sauce **149**

    5-a-day toad-in-the-hole **106–9**

    grating **88**

    grilled bread with tomato and fried garlic **86**

    magical chicken and Parmesan soup with pappardelle **143**

    not-your-average tomato salad **67**

    spiced tomato sauce **156–7**

    summer courgettes with tomatoes and ricotta **81**

    tomato and courgette loaf with spiced tomato chutney **154–5**

    tomato salsa **81**

    tomato sauces **24, 83, 149, 156–7**

    za'atar parathas with grated tomato **28–31**

toum: broad bean and herb salad with toum **195**

    buckwheat-battered fish with toum and pickled chillies **193**

    vampire-slaying toum **190**

tuna: baked orzo puttanesca **114**

turmeric: tamarind, greens and mung beans with turmeric oil **38–9**

    turmeric cashews **92**

U

upside-down lemon, maple and vanilla pudding with lemon-maple butter **218–21**

V

vampire-slaying toum **190**

vanilla: upside-down lemon, maple and vanilla pudding with lemon-maple butter **218–21**

vegetables: any grilled veg with mustard and Parmesan dressing **166**

    crudités **64**

    (that one bag of) mixed veggies and potato fritters with harissa **196–7**

Verena's road trip cookies **224–5**

vermicelli rice noodles: funky faloodeh **214–15**

vindaloo, spicy pulled pork **110–13**

Y

yellow split pea purée with buttered onions and caper salsa **34**

yoghurt: beyond potato salad **165**

    celebration rice with lamb, chicken and garlic yoghurt **144–5**

    grilled courgettes with warm yoghurt and saffron butter **75**

    soda bread with figs, star anise and orange **41**

    very giant giant couscous cake **48–9**

    yoghurt rice with chana dal and curry leaf oil **42–3**

Z

za'atar: peas, tahini and za'atar **182**

    za'atar parathas with grated tomato **28–31**

    za'atar pesto **140–1**

    za'atar salmon and tahini **119**

Acknowledgements

If there's one thing that's apparent in these pages, and for any future stories that the Test Kitchen has to tell, it is that OTK is made up of a team of individuals who each bring to the table their unique quirks and attributes. We cook and bake, style and photograph, write and publish, but more than anything we work together and the OTK would not exist were it not for the efforts of everyone involved. Beyond this, we feel super lucky to have worked with a multitude of talents within their trade, and for this we extend our gratitude.

For the design, a massive thank you to Caz Hildebrand, the creative mastermind behind the edgy cover and whimsical book name 'SHELF LOVE'. You truly brought our visions to life with your out-of-the-box thinking and daring splashes of colour. And to Ashlea O'Neill for her design contribution as well. Also a big high five to Wei Tang, for your props, plants and virtual hugs.

For the photography, many thanks to Elena Heatherwick and her partner in crime Lesley Lau, who captured the Test Kitchen vibes so beautifully. They also provided plenty of giggles throughout the shoot and took home all the leftovers, and for this we are very appreciative.

We're super grateful to the team at Ebury, especially Celia Palazzo for leading the project and Emily Brickell for swiftly making sure we stayed on track. We also extend our thanks to Joel Rickett, Lizzy Gray, Sarah Bennie, Stephenie Naulls, Annie Lee and Catherine Ngwong. Across continents we say a huge thank you to Aaron Wehner, Jennifer Sit, Kim Witherspoon, Maria Zizka, Jen Wang, Kim Tyner, Mark McCauslin, Windy Dorresteyn, Kate Tyler and Jana Branson.

Much love and multiple hugs to the team at Gemma Bell, especially Gemma, Jen and Millie, for adding such wonderful energy to the OTK momentum.

As always, thank you to Mark Hutchinson and Felicity Rubinstein for their support and guidance throughout.

To Nina Tolstrup, we are so grateful to have found you . . . and for the Test Kitchen makeover!

Lastly we'd like to thank Cornelia Staeubli and Noam Bar for their unconditional support in all things OTK.

Noor's acknowledgements

Thank you to my parents, Salah and Vanessa Murad, my two halves of two very different worlds whose unconditional love and support has shaped who I am today. And of course to my sister, Farah Murad.

A huge thanks to the OTK team: to Gitai Fisher, my work partner-in-crime turned brother, whose honesty and strength of character means he won't be rid of me any time soon. The OTK would not be, were it not for you, habibti. To Verena Lochmuller, the most clever pastry chef I have come across, whose passion and talent speaks volumes. You put a smile on my face every day with your kindness, humour and daily meows. To Ixta Belfrage, for being an all-round badass and a pleasure to learn from over the last 3 years. To Tara Wigley and Sami Tamimi, for letting me come into my own via team *Falastin*! To Chaya Pugh, whose jovial spirit brightens even the gloomiest of days. To Claudine Boulstridge, for her support from afar and her array of farm animal photos including pheasants, chicks and llamas. To Cornelia, for finding my CV in her inbox many moons ago and for carving my place in the Ottolenghi family. To all the individuals who have left their mark at the Test Kitchen over the last decade, and all the influences yet to come: the OTK is, and always will be, an accumulation of voices harmoniously in sync.

Much love to my rock Anosha Watson, who believes in me (a little bit) more than I believe in myself and pushes me (a lotta bit) beyond my own limitations. I don't know where I'd be without you.

To my oldest and dearest friend Maram Jaberi, who I carry with me through every life event. Thank you to you and your family for instigating my life-long love affair with Persian cuisine.

To Josh Meehan, the most rewarding surprise of 2020, thank you for your unwavering love and support.

To Celia, Joel, Emily and the whole team at Ebury, many thanks for bringing the OTK vision to life.

To the creative stars Elena Heatherwick, Caz Hildebrand, Nina Tolstrup and Wei Tang: it truly has been a pleasure working with you. The same goes to Gemma Bell and Jen, for being such an awesome force to work with and be around.

To my two London head chefs Shalom and Daniel, now friends for whom I have the utmost respect, thank you for taking a punt on this sassy girl from Bahrain.

Most importantly, a big shukran to Yotam, for being the beating heart of the Test Kitchen, an unwavering source of encouragement and inspiration and a leader who will constantly strive to push his team forward.

Shelf Love notes

OTK

10 9 8 7 6 5 4 3 2 1

Ebury Press, an imprint of Ebury Publishing,
20 Vauxhall Bridge Road,
London, SW1V 2SA

Ebury Press is part of the Penguin Random House group of companies
whose addresses can be found at global.penguinrandomhouse.com

Penguin
Random House
UK

First published by Ebury Press in 2021
www.penguin.co.uk

A CIP catalogue record for this book is available from the British Library

Design: Caz Hildebrand
Photography: Elena Heatherwick
Prop styling: Wei Tang

ISBN: 978-1-52-910948-1

Colour origination by Altaimage Ltd, London
Printed and bound by Graphicom S.r.l

Penguin Random House is committed to a sustainable future for our
business, our readers and our planet. This book is made from Forest
Stewardship Council® certified paper.

OTTOLENGHI TEST KITCHEN

SHELF ⇒ LOVE ⚬

Yotam Ottolenghi
Noor Murad

THE PERFECT INTERACTIVE COMPANION TO THE BOOK

A GIFT FROM THE OTTOLENGHI TEST KITCHEN
All of the recipes at your fingertips, wherever you are

BROWSE
Access all the recipes online from anywhere

SEARCH
Find your perfect recipe by ingredient or browse through the chapters

FAVOURITES
Create your own list of go-to recipes and have them at your fingertips, whether shopping on the way home or looking for recipe ideas during a weekend away

TO UNLOCK YOUR ACCESS VISIT BOOKS.OTTOLENGHI.CO.UK

CONTAINS:

OTK lunchbox, OTK tea towel, dried chickpeas, dried green mung beans, chana dal, black limes and dried ancho chillies

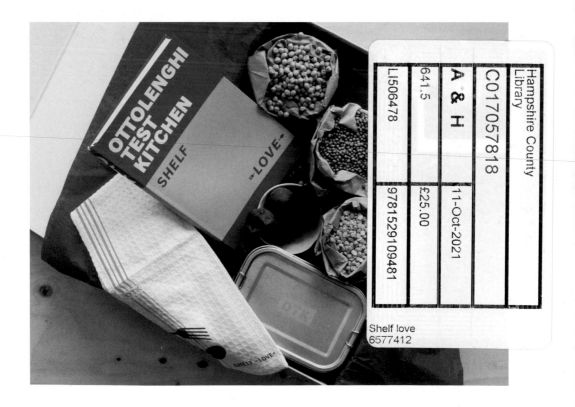